PHILLIP HODSON is Britain's best known 'agony uncle'. In the past seven years he has advised countless people about their personal and sexual problems through his broadcasts on LBC, one of London's commercial radio stations, and through the columns of the *Daily Star*. He has pursued this dual career of counsellor and journalist since 1974 when he became one of the first single men to be accepted by the Marriage Guidance Council for training.

As well as editing *Forum* for eight years, Phillip has written articles for numerous newspapers and magazines, including the *Observer* and *Cosmopolitan*, and is at present hosting a late-night talk show on LBC and finishing his forthcoming book on Wagner.

Men...

An investigation into the emotional male

Phillip Hodson

ARIEL BOOKS
BRITISH BROADCASTING CORPORATION

For Anne Hooper,
Alfred Clement Hodson

The BBC Continuing Education Television series, *Men . . .*,
first transmitted on BBC2 from January 1984, was produced by
Bernard Adams and Lucy Parker.

First published 1984

Published by the British Broadcasting Corporation,
35 Marylebone High Street, London W1M 4AA

Typeset in Linotron Ehrhardt by
Phoenix Photosetting, Chatham
Printed in England by Mackays of Chatham Ltd, Kent

ISBN 0 563 21054 0

Contents

Acknowledgements

I am indebted to Bernard Adams and his BBC colleagues, Lucy Parker and Maggie Winkworth, and to Charles Elton and editor Jennie Allen. Bernard kept me going, Jennie kept me straight and Anne Hooper kept me. The book had many midwives but any errors in the child are mine.

Introduction: Men in Crisis

> 'Men are right in sensing inexorable forces that are undermining their previous claim to natural superiority . . . The conditions we now live in are different from those of any prior civilisation, and they give less support to men's claim of superiority than any other historical era' (Betty Friedan, *The Second Stage*, 1982)

A serious newspaper once asked the exuberant question, 'What do men really want?' to be bluntly answered by one of their female readers, 'Sex and chips'. This may be funny but is it completely false? The respondent made it clear that the men she knew regarded women as sexually attractive cooks—mere servicefolk.

Some men want women to get out of paid employment:

> 'To come down to one detail: the materialistic craving for things, the extra car, the second TV, the exotic holiday, are forcing many young women to neglect their young families and fill jobs which should be held by young men . . . Shall we ever return to the basic principles of father providing and mother caring?' (Letter, *Times*, 17/5/1983)

More than one man believes certain jobs are inherently masculine:

> 'In the present serious economic conditions, it is amazing that the Engineering Council has decided to designate 1984 as *Girls Into Engineering Year*.
> I would have thought that it was obvious to anyone that engineering is a natural job for a boy, it always has been and always will be. With over three million unemployed at

the present time of which many thousands must be boys desperate for the opportunity to train as engineers, this proposal ... is ridiculous.' (Letter, *New Civil Engineer*, quoted *Guardian* 6/6/1983)

Now it may be true that men as a sex want women to retire to the kitchen sink and abandon to them the serious business of engineering the country's economy. But just suppose this does not happen. Suppose some women with the relevant qualifications insist on becoming engineers; that many women continue to resist being treated as nothing more than sexually attractive cooks and that the nine million, eleven thousand women currently in paid employment (as of December 1982) refuse to yield up their jobs to men, even if their families can afford the loss of income? Just suppose that the unemployment figure for men alone rises to four million and stays there? What then? Aren't men going to be left with problems in their relationships with women and at work which they can only solve by re-assessing their masculinity?

This book sets out to examine some of these fundamental questions. How do men feel about life in a world peopled by women who are their equals? What are the problems this raises for them? Can men adjust internally to such a situation without undergoing psychological frustration? And if some of my answers to these questions seem critical of men, bear in mind that I apply them first and foremost to myself and only wish to assist my sex, through a re-examination of our identities, to longer life, liberty and the pursuit of inner happiness.

1 The Fragile Male

'Sexually men are already under attack. Shortly this attack will spread and the effect on men is going to be devastating' (Helen Mirren, quoted by Derek Bowskill and Anthea Linacre, *Men: The Sensitive Sex*, 1977)

'The man, in his rough work in the open world, must encounter all peril and trial: to him, therefore, must be the failure, the offence, the inevitable error: often he must be wounded, or subdued; often misled; and *always* hardened' (John Ruskin, *Sesame and Lilies*, 1882)

'I am now 49 years of age, unmarried and a complete failure. I generally feel I have wasted all the good years. Nothing anyone says will make me think otherwise until I have achieved a measure of success as I understand it . . .' (D.H., London)

'Men comprise by far the greater number of successful suicides' (Jack Nichols, *Men's Liberation*, 1975)

One of the primary reasons for the modern male crisis is the fact that women have been so successful in identifying the female crisis. The 'new women' no longer want the 'old' traditional men and constantly lambast them for their chauvinistic views, though usually underplaying the point that chauvinism traps men as well as women in roles which they may not want. But even non-feminists seem to be rejecting the accepted male stereotype:

'Increasingly, women want a kind, considerate, humorous partner, not a dominant provider' (Questionnaire, *Daily Express*, February 1982).

Sociologists like Dr Robert Chester of Hull University contribute further evidence from the female population generally:

> 'In my survey of the marital satisfaction of 10,000 UK women, we found that nearly all were highly satisfied with their husbands as breadwinners and supporters but up to one third complained that their partners were inept as companions and ineffectual as confidants . . . which we know is a fundamental cause of divorce . . .' (*Intimate Relations*, BBC *Horizon* Documentary, 1982).

Statistics from the divorce courts underscore this criticism of men since for every man in Britain who divorces his wife, three women divorce their husbands. And perhaps society in general is sending a message to men by employing more brain and un-employing brawn in the modern, push-button, increasingly 'feminine' economy. Who values brute strength in a land of automation and increased leisure? Who can ignore the psychological challenge presented by male unemployment when industrial de-manning so clearly leads to mental un-manning?

> 'Unemployed people are twice as likely to become mentally ill as those in jobs and the most vulnerable group is composed of middle-aged married men with children and financial commitments . . . factors involved are . . . the work ethic, financial strain and being male, middle-aged and working class . . .' (Report on SSRC and Medical Research Council Study, Sheffield, 1977–1983).

Emasculation through loss of work is proving to be deeply destructive to men psychologically, but I see little evidence that they are putting their energy into side-stepping the consequences or even investing in what we might call 're-masculation'. At present, they are sitting on their thrones as the kingdom collapses, demanding, Canute-fashion, that the tide of female employment be halted because they cannot cope with wet feet and refusing to accept that the traditional economy of metal-bashing by horny-handed sons of toil is in decline. And so are its more dogmatic attitudes and values.

> 'With the continuing decline of Britain's traditional manu-facturing base and the growth of the service sector, there will almost certainly be relatively few manual workers left

by the end of the century.' (Ian Bradley, *The English Middle Classes*. . ., 1980).

A revaluation of masculinity ought surely to be as helpful to men as feminism has been to women, since 1950s masculinity is obviously unsuited to the vastly altered conditions of the 1980s. While women have responded to new developments in contraception and household automation on the one hand, and changes in the economy and the application of the workforce on the other (redefining their social role in the process), men as sexual theorists have been left standing on the line.

Notice what men have *not* been doing by recalling some of women's recent successes. Since World War II, women have demonstrated that the proper study of womankind is woman. In the universities, many courses have evolved under the generic title of 'Women's Studies'. Publishing groups such as Virago have popularised feminism with texts new and old while generally refusing to print any document authored by a male. Women have developed a system of ideas to explain their difficulties in marriage, work and sex which depend for their validity on the assumption that women are the sensitive underclass. In this respect, they have hijacked the primary virtues of humanity for themselves. A bond has been forged between women asserting that not only is sisterhood powerful, it is personal. Women talk to women and women feel for each other. They have not yet achieved all their ambitions, including equal representation in Parliament and the professions, but even women who repudiate sexual politics identify with the move towards articulate self-determination.

By contrast, men have re-thought next to nothing and we have allowed our prestige to decline by default. The most graphic illustration of this for me was perhaps the scene in a large feminist bookshop when one of the BBC's researchers asked to be directed to the shelves of books about men. The assistant regarded her as though she'd asked about Martians and pointed out a tiny shelf at ground level at the back of the shop. Fortunately, not all feminists are so incurious. In 1973, Sheila Rowbotham appealed to men to explore the roots of their own compulsive behaviour for the benefit of all:

'. . . I sensed something very complicated was going on in the heads of men who were about my age. It's for them to write about this. I wish they would very soon' (*Woman's Consciousness, Man's World*, 1973).

If Rowbotham was correct and men were beginning to look inside themselves at this time, then something seems to have inhibited publication since the results to date have hardly troubled the bookshelves. And yet women crave to be let into the secret of the armoured male mind, a prime reason for this being, of course, to assist in the further development of their own consciousness. As pioneering feminist Betty Friedan has suggested (*The Second Stage*, 1982), there cannot be enduring women's liberation without men's liberation. There can only be sexual warfare.

It is said that men enjoy the game of war provided they think they are going to win. Have they, therefore, been too intimidated in advance by women's successes to attempt a counter-attack, or have they simply been outflanked? In either case the competitive male ego has clearly failed to meet the challenge. As women run on ahead, men shuffle on the spot, take pride in their blinkers and pass the time by kicking each other when down, regardless of the ultimate risk of disqualification from the human race. If women have really irrevocably redefined themselves *away* from the old order of men, so men must alter course or lose touch.

Naturally, the fact that women are critical of men cuts no ice by itself since traditional men do not defer to women's judgements and rather suspect that what is good for women is bad for men. But what if it could be shown that traditional masculine values play their part in damaging men mentally and physically, lie behind a great many divorce cases and possibly shorten the male lifespan? Would not self-preservation at least cause men to change tack?

If so, consider the available evidence. It still seems that, on the whole, men like women. The human race is 90 per cent heterosexual. Men wish to go to bed with women in preference to any alternative. Practically all adult males who can be married *are* married. They actually have every incentive to be so since research shows that men *without* women have higher rates of suicide, insanity, cancer and coronary thrombosis than those who enjoy lasting relationships. The statistics, for once, are staggering. About 93 per cent of people get married in Britain. Of the men who remain single, twice as many are likely to kill themselves as married males of the same age, four times as many are likely to enter a mental hospital, one and a half times as many may suffer a coronary and twice as many are likely to die of cancer of the throat or mouth.

Evidence from America, where divorce is even more prevalent

than in Britain, warns of increased risks threatening men after the break-up of their marriages. In one divorce study, Dr Bloom of the University of Colorado shows that separated and divorced American males are about nine times more likely to be admitted to a psychiatric hospital than are married men. He points out that this ratio of nine to one is a very big number indeed, of the same startling degree as that applying to the incidence of lung cancer between smokers and non-smokers. Moreover, the mortality rate in the USA is two to three times higher among separated and divorced men from practically any major disease – lung cancer, tuberculosis, coronary disease and arthritis – than it is among the successfully married. Divorced men also die more frequently from road accidents, suicide and alcoholism than married men.

For over five years, Professor James Lynch of the University of Baltimore has studied this area of male mortality. He concludes that for men under 70, the death rate is between two and ten times higher for the divorced and separated than for the married men. Professor Marvin Stein of New York's Mount Sinai Medical Center now believes that the body's immune system, the mechanism with which we normally combat disease, is the element which is broken down by the stress of divorce and separation in particular in relation to cancer, heart disease, arthritis and diabetes. In addition, Peter Ambrose, John Harper and Richard Pemberton have shown in their study of 92 divorced British couples that the career prospects of men can be seriously damaged by divorce (*Men Beyond Marriage*, 1983).

Such evidence makes it seem even more bizarre, therefore, that men have so far invested minimal resources in making themselves desirable to the new generation of women. Instead, they continue to risk their lives and prosperity by holding stubbornly to the old manly stereotype.

If you ask about this stereotype, as I have been doing lately, you come up with some droll answers. One man even told me that it was central to any definition of masculinity that men never peed sitting down. A popular quiz for masculinity is mentioned by Edmund White, author of *A Boy's Own Story* (1982):

'(1) Look at your nails (a girl extends her fingers, a boy cups his in his upturned palm); (2) Look up (a girl lifts just her eyes, a boy throws back his whole head); (3) Light a match (a girl strikes away from her body, a boy toward) . . . A man crosses his legs by resting an ankle on his knee; a sissy

> drapes one leg over the other. A man never gushes; men are either silent or loud . . .'

The more typical responses were that manliness meant 'seeking power', 'being a worker', 'squashing weak emotions', 'providing a living for the family', 'taking the lead in sex', 'needing more sex than the woman', 'being responsible because stronger' and 'taking the most important decisions'. In America, many of these British answers were echoed in Shere Hite's *Hite Report on Male Sexuality*, a 1981 survey of 7239 men aged between 13 and 97:

> 'My father taught me typical male macho stuff about being a man. Men don't cry. Men don't show emotion. Men provide. Men are the stronger sex. Women are weak physically and emotionally. Honour and duty above all else. Sports, hard work were masculine. Arts, music and the fine professions (with the exception of law and medicine) were suspect, if not downright feminine. A woman was to be indulged; was the only proper sex object; was for tending the home and raising the family; worked outside the home if necessary but never supported a man worth his salt. A real man would rather die than show more emotion to another man than a handshake.'

> 'Work hard, pay your bills, keep out of debt, owe no man, beat the system, pay cash, be clean, stand up for yourself, be formidable to your enemies, hit back, to be a man is to be a success, don't let women get in your way or stop you from being a success, don't let love or a woman dominate your life.'

> 'Fight, fuck and make a lot of money . . .'

In countries like Brazil, it is the myth of *machismo* which is held up as the ideal code of behaviour for all males and is tied up with one physical activity in particular:

> '[It] is almost synonymous with maleness – but a maleness which is based almost solely upon dominance in the sexual act' (*New Society*, 5/5/1983).

A cheap but nevertheless telling blow can be aimed at such definitions by suggesting that anyone who makes so much noise belittling gentle feelings must have rather a lot of them to hide. To observers it often seems that tough guys protest too much. Secondly, it is actually only two thirds of his emotions that a man is enjoined to conceal since the rules of the game permit him to express violent anger and rage. If, as the advertising world would have it, 'real men don't eat quiche', it can only be because they need raw red meat to fuel their aggression. And finally, there is a wry paradox in the fact that what the 'strong' male sometimes lacks is strength of personality to confess to incompetence in the face of life's inevitable setbacks. Moreover, male culture enforces this as one of its most important characteristics, so that it is possible to conclude that official manhood actually incorporates moral weakness. When put like this, I think few men would be proud to uphold the concept.

Men feel bound to a considerable extent by what they have been told are the 'facts' governing the differences between the sexes, especially those reports from sociobiologists, hereditarians and rat doctors asserting that men are constitutionally more powerful than women both mentally and physically. This is frequently propaganda.

In general, the differences between the sexes are fewer and less dramatic than most people believe (see Table I). As you might expect of creatures belonging to the same species, men and women have identical central nervous systems. They feel pleasure and pain in exactly the same way. Although the sexes have differing hormonal balances (and in general males are prone to be more aggressive), no one has yet suggested that little boys lack the capacity to feel love and affection. As time goes by, however, boys are socialised to express more aggression than tenderness and girls the opposite, with two rather striking consequences. Boys when they attain manhood suffer from broad inhibition across a spectrum of emotion even though the underlying feelings clearly do not disappear. And girls are taught to repress their ambitious and competitive behaviour thereby evading a destructive measure of personal stress. In their late teens, many boys who find the assertive male role to be uncongenial retreat into shyness since they are not encouraged to talk out their self-doubts. And although teenage women can experience similar problems because they are not encouraged to make personal initiatives in this area, they are at least spared the performance burden with which men are saddled.

It is a pity that women's abilities are not more fully used since there is evidence to suggest they are constitutionally better

Table I Sex differences and similarities (after Tavris and Offir, *The Longest War: Sex Differences in Perspective*, 1977)

Abilities

General intelligence	No difference
Verbal ability	Females excel on some tests
Quantitative ability	Males excel on some tests (after puberty)
Creativity	Females excel on verbal creativity, otherwise no difference
Cognitive style	No difference
Visual-spatial ability	Males excel on some tests (after puberty)
Physical abilities	Males more muscular; males more vulnerable to illness, disease; females excel on some tests where manual dexterity important but findings ambiguous

Personality characteristics

Sociability and love	Evidence that boys play in larger groups but in a 'tribal' rather than 'personal' fashion; men fall in love more quickly than women and out of love with more difficulty
Empathy	Conflicting evidence
Emotionality	Evidence that boys grow less able to express feelings as childhood progresses, whereas girls entrench this skill; men poor at intimacy compared to women
Dependence	Strong evidence that all humans interdepend, need physical touch and verbal communication; no evidence men need this less than women
Nurturance	No overall difference in altruism; good evidence that fathers can be as nurturant towards children as mothers; men less comfortable about admitting this fact
Aggressiveness*	Males more aggressive from pre-school on

* The aggressivity of males and passivity of females is heavily reinforced by cultural conditioning to the point where sorting out the impact of nature and nurture becomes extremely difficult.

equipped than men to cope with stress. Indeed, it would not be stretching a point to suggest that, right across the board, women are the more biologically successful sex.

For a start, and I cannot think of a more telling argument, men die earlier (see Table II).

Table II

Expectation of life in years (UK) at birth (*Social Trends*, No. 13, 1983)

Year	1901	1931	1951	1961	1971	1979
Males	48.0	58.0	66.2	67.9	68.8	70.2
Females	51.6	62.4	71.2	73.8	75.0	76.2

In America, the difference in the life expectancy of men and women at birth is an average of eight years in favour of the latter.

During this century, in both countries, growing numbers of women have been committed to the workforce even though there is no comparable evidence to show that men have taken on more of the childcare and domestic duties. Indeed, there is evidence from Scandinavia, Russia and the USA to show that men have routinely evaded these duties (Table III). Therefore, we are forced to conclude that women have a capacity to endure the strains of two separate labour tasks while still increasing their life expectancy both absolutely and in relation to men. I grant that few women so far have had to cope with the pressures of 'top' jobs. Men still jealously occupy most such positions. But when you look at the coping aptitudes of women in general, you might be forgiven for coming to regard men as comparatively frail. In fact male fragility is evident from birth onwards. Five per cent more male babies are born each year than females but more males die in the first year of life. In the USA in 1978, this death rate was 15.3 per 1000 male babies in the first year but only 12.9 per 1000 in the first year for females.

Men are more susceptible to disease than women; they suffer more from colds and 'flu and when a novel pneumonia arrives, such as Legionnaire's Disease, three times as many men as women fall victim to it. According to figures recorded by psychologist Dr Joyce Brothers (*What Every Woman Should Know About Men*, 1982), more men than women die from 14 out of the leading 15 'sudden' causes of death:

'heart disease, cancer, cerebrovascular disease, accidents, influenza and pneumonia, conditions of early infancy, diabetes mellitus, arterio-sclerosis, bronchitis, emphysema and asthma, cirrhosis, congenital anomalies, homicide, nephritis-nephrosis, peptic ulcer and suicide'.

Women only suffer more fatality from diabetes but not by much and men tend to experience greater associated kidney damage with this complaint.

Table III Men's contribution to housework (after Brothers, *What Every Woman Should Know About Men*, 1982)

USA (survey by Batten, Barton, Durstine & Osborne and Doyle, Dane & Bernbach and A. C. Nielson)
Three out of five US wives do paid work. Only 19 per cent said this was pure choice; 81 per cent said the family needed the money. However, 71 per cent of the husbands said their wives worked by choice and 80 per cent of the husbands said they expected the woman to cope with all shopping and household chores, including the childcare. While 35 per cent of husbands agreed that vacuum cleaning at home was an acceptable male chore, only 27 per cent of them had ever pushed a machine across the carpet.
The working wife spends an average of 26 hours per week on housework. Her husband spends 26 minutes.
A three-year-long study of 1400 dual career families with children under the age of 11 showed that only one father in five helped out with the childcare.

Denmark (survey by Ministry of Labour)
This study found that the working wife spends an average of 21 hours per week on housework.
Her husband spends one hour 45 minutes.

Soviet Union (survey by Ministry of Labour)
The non-working wife is practically non-existent, yet wives are still expected by husbands to do all shopping, cooking, childcare and, above all, queueing for supplies, while their partners watch TV and drink with male companions.

In addition, women are more efficient at using and maintaining their bodies. Since they have more body insulation and can metabolise their fat reserves better than men, they have more *long-term* energy. Consider the following facts regarding stamina and age-related physical efficiency:

● the female capacity for exercise exceeds that of the male;

● a woman aged 60 can exercise up to 90 per cent of the capacity she had when 20. A man of 60 can exercise only up to 60 per cent of his capacity when 20 (quoted in Brothers, 1982);

● women remain warmer in winter and cooler in summer because of the more even distribution of their sweat glands;

● men don't have energy reserves on the same scale as women, since women have more fat.

One advantage of this, according to Dr Joan Ullyot of the Institute of Health Research in San Francisco, is that in the event of a shipwreck, women are more likely to survive than men! Also, since they can replace blood more quickly and breathe more often, women are more likely to survive accidents, and indeed operations, than men.

In fact, even if we get down to the nitty gritty subject of muscular strength, male partisans have shocks in store. At the West Point military academy, USA, in 1976, it was discovered after a comprehensive series of tests that while young women have only one third of the upper body strength of young men, they have two thirds of the leg strength and *equal* abdominal strength. This is attained despite the male's routine size advantage, so if girls' early puberty were delayed allowing their adolescent growth spurt to continue along with that of the boys, they might retain the height advantage they have over males at ten and therefore achieve corresponding muscular strength.

Anthropologist Ashley Montagu actually thinks the traditional male stereotype should be reversed. In his view, women are without doubt 'biologically superior' to men since they can:

'endure all sorts of devitalizing conditions better than men: starvation, exposure, fatigue, shock, illness and the like. The female is constitutionally stronger than the male and only muscularly less powerful. She has greater stamina.' (quoted in Brothers, 1982).

So if men really want to be literal providers, i.e. hunters, they do indeed have certain in-built advantages since they are taller, heavier and more muscular. But, at the same time, they are more likely to tire, fall sick and suffer from stress. And as one or two male sages have noticed, society is not knee-deep in vacancies for buffalo and reindeer hunters:

'Mankind's greatest problem is that he is caught in the twentieth century with a nature largely shaped by evolution to deal with ice-age problems.' Professor E. O. Williams, Harvard University).

So much for male strength – but what of male aggression? Within living memory, bayonet instruction in the US Marines was punctuated with the following chant:

'Men, what is the spirit of the bayonet?'
'To kill, drill sergeant.'
'Men, will you kill?'
'Yes, drill sergeant.'
'Men, why will you kill?'
'Because we have balls, drill sergeant.'

Some believe it is the production of the male sex hormone, testosterone, by the testes which causes male aggression, but if this is so, why should it be necessary to bolster the tendency with the recitation of ritual poems? Men *are* more violent than women, but the advanced Western world has little daily use for this violence. It has become a problem to cope with at football grounds rather than a guarantee of secure defence on the national frontier. The modern state prefers to kill in professional cold blood. It seems that modern wars will be fought, if at all, by remote control, captained by computer. High levels of manic emotionality will prove militarily counter-productive. So man, the aggressive hunter-killer, is becoming irrelevant. Women can press buttons as easily as men.

Finally, what of male intellectual superiority and its implications for the pattern of men and women's jobs in the future? If you scan the examination returns for England and Wales in recent years you will find that girls are outperforming boys in school:

'. . . there have been very considerable changes in the pattern of [girls'] education in the last 20 years. More pupils of both sexes obtain passes in public examinations now, but the increase for girls has been more rapid than for boys, and girls have now overtaken boys numerically in [CSE and O-level] examinations. At A-level in 1961 boys gaining one or more passes outnumbered girls 3 to 2 but in

1980 figures were approximately 62,000 for boys and 55,000 for girls [a ratio of about 3 to 2.7]' (Report on Secondary Education, Women's National Commission, 1983).

Although boys are at present sitting more exams in maths, physics and computer studies than girls, and girls are conversely dominant in English studies, teachers and educationalists are actively promoting the hard sciences for women, as well as encouraging more women to become head teachers and role leaders in general. When female high performance is expressed in subjects leading to highly paid jobs in new technology, men will have to look to their laurels. After all, when the silicon chips are down, companies will have to employ the best person for the job, regardless of sex. As it is, high performance in school exams and the encouragement of the feminist movement is giving women the opportunity to channel their abilities into preserves formerly occupied solely by men. This will inevitably swell the ranks of women at manager and middle executive level. Women can be just as effective bureaucrats as men.

The credit for these coming changes cannot go to Women's Liberation alone. Women could not have been 'permitted' a vision of liberation on the national scale unless the wider economy newly required their participation as equals in the business of production. It is not just because feminists have penned complaints that sex equality is arriving. Society itself has prompted the change in order to tap the neglected pool of female brain-power. The implication for patriarchal order is obvious. Even if 'manly' values of competition and exploitation continue to flourish in the modern world, can men as a sex be certain that they will supply the personnel who practise them? Can they be so positive that Margaret Thatcher is not a harbinger?

A further consideration follows from this in connection with the demands of modern capitalism. In most econometric models, Western Europe faces mass unemployment of more than 12 million until the year 2000 and who knows what beyond. Traditional men still define themselves in terms of their work: 'I am a builder . . . an engineer . . . a journalist . . . a salesmen . . .'. But when their work no longer defines itself in terms of them, commanding their dismissal, do men simply cease to exist or must they revalue their identities? Since it is folly to blame all the world's unemployment on the unemployed, surely it is equally foolish of unemployed men to go on regarding themselves as workers first and foremost when that is what they so poignantly are not?

'Sitting on his front porch in the sun is David Hunt. At 32 he has not worked for three years. Labouring jobs are now going to 17-year-olds who, he says, are paid much less than the going rate for an adult.

What does he do all day?

"Be a woman", comes the reply.' (*Guardian*, 30/5/1983).

If only he *could* be like a woman and define himself as the person he undoubtedly is, or as the son, husband, father or friend he might also be. Perhaps then he could enjoy more self-respect, acquire more self-confidence, suffer less depression and cope more effectively with society's cruelty towards him. Unemployment is a curse; but so too is a dead-end job. Unemployment is also *leisure*. Down through the centuries, political theorists have proposed paid mass leisure as the goal of civilisation. It is obscene that rich countries should pay so little to their redundant workers. But those redundant workers are the new leisure class, like it or not. And men liberated from what used to be called 'wage slavery' can recover an important part of their identity, like it or not. It is one of the arguments of this book that they should recover more. After all, why should they support the very values of masculinity which have made them redundant?

So far I have written about the social context of men's feelings and the economic overview. I have been impersonal, presenting my thesis in what I hope to be a 'winning' form and using, without scruple, the one argument which I think will touch a masculine nerve – the prick of self-interest. What I have not yet done, and will do in the next chapter, is to describe any of the internal feelings (or rather the suppression of these) which men bound up in this modern male crisis experience.

2 The Emotional Switch-off

'"He was crying", said Lucy-Ann, in sheer amazement that a boy of fourteen could do such a thing' (Enid Blyton, *The Ship of Adventure*, 1950)

'They are ashamed of their own sensitivity to suffering and love because they have been taught to regard these as feminine. They are afraid of becoming feminine because this means that other men will despise them, we will despise them and they will despise themselves' (Sheila Rowbotham, *Woman's Consciousness, Man's World*, 1973)

'Generally I don't enjoy talking about my emotions. I much prefer current events. She often complains that I don't talk about my feelings enough. The problem, I tell her, is that I don't have enough feelings. My emotional response is turned very low, whether by genetics or environment or both. I'm not a reactive person . . .' (quoted by Shere Hite, *The Hite Report on Masculinity*, 1981)

'men bleed too' (feminist graffito)

A baby boy at birth is pleasure-bound. Obstetrician William Masters used to devise a game with himself: 'Can I get the cord cut before the kid has an erection?' From birth onwards, the boy-child appears to be more restless and active than the girl, which is usually attributed to the influence of pre-natal hormones. He is dubbed 'aggressive', but nearly every sign of early assertion meets with parental approval anyway: 'Lively little fellow, isn't he . . . dead wicked . . . a real caution'. Mothers actually exercise boys' limbs more than girls'. At seven weeks old, parents speak more 'roughly' to boys than girls. By the age of three, boys have been taught to laugh at girls' more gentle games and they are very aware to which sex they themselves belong.

According to psychologist Carol Gilligan, this is the time when boys begin to 'disconnect':

> 'I think [it] comes from being brought up by a woman. A little girl is very close to her mother. A little boy has to separate himself from his mother to feel like a boy.' (*In A Different Voice: Psychological Theory and Women's Development*, 1982).

The crucial distance or absence of the typical father figure at this time ('busy or tired') contributes to the boy's sense of loss. To be masculine, he must fight free from his mother, from which he learns that it is wrong to 'cling'. (When I was stung by a bee at the age of six and ran for comfort to my mother she teased me with the words 'You'll die after it . . .' because I was a boy and ought to behave like a man.) And then he must endeavour to become like his father whom he doesn't know and with whom he cannot compete on equal terms. From this he learns that it is right to become 'aloof' if only in the interests of not being unmasked as a frightened fraud. (For a long time if I didn't know the answer to a question I would, like my father, change the subject . . .)

So, during infancy there is a change in the boy's pleasurable consciousness towards a condition of wariness. He has learned not to trust his subjective feelings. They are not factual. He must be rational. He must be objective, like his father. He must be impersonal, unlike his mother. He must be competitive with fellow males in order to achieve power. Such potency must be hard, external, visible, measurable, or it is effeminate and does not count. Men must manoeuvre openly to make their mark on the world. Inner power is a self-contradiction because it is not asserted over rivals. And the essence of masculine potency is that it robs another of status: I win, you lose. All of which is built on the original childhood misconception that it is an asset to be emotionally invulnerable. As the years go by, this causes the boy-child to reject physical touch from his parents and to cease to give voice to inner fears. If you don't use a skill you tend to lose it: already by the age of nine boys are poor at communicating with their peers. They prefer to talk about their play, which is safe, rather than about themselves; girls tend to do the opposite.

By early teenage, boys are well into the important business of finding their place in the masculine pecking order. They are preoccupied with the deeds of their male contemporaries. They join that lifelong team or gang where they always hope to impress. They fight, engage in contests of conspicuous glucose consumption, they bully, cajole and browbeat their weaker brethren. Emotionally, they learn the happy knack of making themselves feel better by making others feel worse. Those males who are less adequate – usually the fat, the thin and the poorly co-ordinated – keep their heads down as best they can. They probably know what happened to 'Piggy' at the hands of his 'friends' in William Golding's novel *Lord of the Flies* (1954).

The arrival of puberty is disconcerting to strong and weak alike. Calculations of the existing balance of power are upset. If you reflect that the emotional development of boy-children is often analogous to the attempt to build self-sufficient Sherman tanks, think what a sudden handicap it is for them to want and need sexual fulfilment from the opposed, indeed the 'enemy' sex. No wonder early encounters sometimes consist of boys treating girls like Space Invader Machines on which it is necessary to compile stupendous scores. It takes many years for some men to accept their sexuality and to place it in the context of a man-woman relationship. They find it very difficult to dissociate sex from a lust for power *over* the woman in a contest which is essentially *against* other men. There is frequent stress on a quantifiable performance ('eight times . . . eight hours . . . eight women . . . eight towns . . . eighty-eight different positions . . .') in descriptions redolent of a raid by the SAS. Other men never progress beyond seeing sex as all-action 'genital theft' from the woman, in the sense of stealing an advantage over her by obtaining her consent, a perfect contradiction in terms.

By the time men reach manhood, they are often specialists in 'nonspeak' about important emotional issues, whether to parents (with whom they are regularly in conflict) or to friends. They are fickle in their romantic relationships or eat their hearts out with a crippling shyness largely concealed from the world. The enormous 'puissance' of masculinity is by now so unstable that any personal rejection will bring the house down like a pack of cards. Therefore none must be risked. 'I haven't spoken to a female in a non-work situation since I was 11,' admitted one 22-year-old, public-school educated, computer-designer.

Yet most men do get married. For many, this is *the* maturing process which sees the resumption of emotional growth. But for some, the marital motive is mainly to extend power over a woman and a family. In sad cases, such men oscillate in behaviour between being hectoring bullies and incommunicative mutes, having come to rely on there being a 'defective' female beside them to bolster their notion of masculinity. (The most telling example was the chap who complained to a counsellor: 'My wife is frigid and I want her fixed,' only to recoil in horror and secondary impotence when after four weeks of sex therapy she became orgasmic and therefore 'difficult'.)

An occasional secondary motive in getting married is partial regression to childhood, using the wife as a parent-replica (there are many marriages where the adult female is *only* referred to as 'Mother'). Dr Joyce Brothers characterises a man's life from the age of 21 to 35 as 'Divorce Period I' during which he tends to regard himself as the 'superchild' with his wife as the 'mother/mistress' figure. He is seldom aware that his partner has needs of her own, just as the child is unaware of his mother's needs. The divorce usually coincides with the birth of children. (Surveys on both sides of the Atlantic show that the advent of children almost always causes the marital relationship to deteriorate.) For the man it means displacement. He exhibits a bad case of sibling rivalry so to speak. Added to this jealousy are the problems of fatigue, loss of sex and a depressed standard of living. He would prefer to be career-focused (the old struggle against his fellowmen). He knows that if he is not a 'success' by the time he is 35, he never will be, and at this moment he may well decide to opt out domestically in pursuit of sound sleep, bountiful sex and a career of glory.

I feel the underlying reason for such early divorce is the man's inability to relate emotionally on an adult-to-adult basis. How could he? The last time he related emotionally was on a child-to-mother basis. Since then he has been left out in the cold. There are several alternatives to the marriage scenario as described by Dr Brothers, including the quite common British picture of the husband as father-figure deigning to marry a child-woman who reveres him as a cross between the *Encyclopaedia Britannica* and a High Court Judge. But again, there is very little adult-to-adult exchange and such marriages generally expire in the time it takes the woman to complete her education and commence an independent career.

Marriages of unequals are nearly always doomed. One of the constant demands of women on men at the moment is for men to express themselves more. Silence is power, although of a brittle order. If the man insists on silent power, if he seeks dominance by right, if he takes refuge in the external rights and obligations of matrimony (one of which is sexual intercourse), he'll probably get left. He certainly won't get loved. It is often at this moment in the voice of deepest outrage that he announces to the world:

> 'My wife abandoned me for absolutely no reason whatso-ever. I was a good husband . . . a good provider . . . a good father [meaning provider] . . . and good at DIY around the house . . .'

Alas for him, all this would no longer be good enough if it meant that he wasn't good at intimacy, reading his family's moods, giving his time to childcare (not just his cash) and good at 'servicing' his marriage emotionally.

If he manages to survive this first great Divorce Period, a husband is immediately beset by a second era of marital instability as he enters his 'pivotal' 40s. Because men don't live as long as women, they reach middle age earlier (at 35 rather than 40). As a consequence, says Brothers, men arrive sooner at the moment in life when they start to count the years 'remaining' rather than the ones that 'lie ahead'. As for marriage, men get more wedded to the institution itself than the day-to-day reality (and as Groucho Marx once said 'Who wants to live in an institution, anyway?'). They are often bored by the sexual chores. They could also be career-disillusioned at this point, understanding that they will never now make it to the top. Facing this as a truth probably means embracing depression. Depression is a vital learning mechanism, allowing feelings to catch up with events, a time when you realise with painful consciousness the vital discrepancy between the facts in life and your pretences about them. But to keep depressions at bay, many men revert to childhood, hoping against hope that the teenage lovers they take will somehow keep them youthful too. To this end, they sacrifice home and marriage, abandoning in the process a partnership of some 20 years' standing. In parenthesis let us add that such doom is not inevitable. Even in the most conventional families feelings of despair can be safely voiced and that triggers the healing process. But who doesn't know of a divorce caused because a middle-aged man has run off with a woman almost young enough to be his daughter?

When a man has survived all these emotional phases he only has to face retirement. Now the man who has taken his full identity from his job and internalised the notion of 'work' as a constant approach to existence gets very stuck. For a couple of years at 60 or 65 he may 'work' at the garden, or 'work' at painting the house, or 'work' at playing bridge or golf, or even 'work' at sex, but it doesn't count, there's no pay, no promotion and the reality is that work is no longer required from him. He is instead instructed by society to rest on his internal laurels. For many men this is fine. They have been able through the years to spatchcock together a sense of self-esteem which is independent of making measurable triumphs over male rivals. They *did* manage to acquire the gift of making friendships and to learn how to hold non-competitive conversations with younger people, to preserve their health and to enjoy the home for its own sake instead of seeing it as a place in which to make pit-stops from work. Yet alas for others, what they have been taught about the danger of emotion destroys their very lives. It is too late to open up. They cannot find re-inforcement from within themselves. They only value tangible material and power rewards. So in effect it is impossible for them to find happiness, since happiness itself is an emotion. And emotions are dangerous. Catch 22; aged 65. In a short space of months, such men die the workless death.

If this seems an unduly black picture of the stages of a man's emotional development and overscathing of man-kind in general, it is worth remembering the admirable, even heroic male qualities, traditionally nurtured and preserved, which it would be folly not to praise. When farmworker Roy Tapping lost his arm in a hay baler and walked half a mile across fields clutching the severed limb in the hope that surgeons would be able to sew it back into place (which they did, June 1983), one humbly admired the stoicism he displayed throughout the ordeal. The surgeon described him as 'amazing, a real hard man, the sort who feels it is almost obligatory to joke about it . . . remarkably composed' (*Guardian*, 29/6/83). It is probably the case that men are conditioned to be good at this sort of thing (though many women are too), and we should give credit where credit is due. The psychological damage starts when men reinforce heroism as an obligatory stereotype for all occasions. It is manly to be a hero if you can. But what is so appalling about being a sissy (sister?) when you can't? It is not in human nature to cope under all circumstances, whatever our sex, for the excellent reason that we are not robots. So why the veto on tears? If Ajax and Achilles could weep, why can't common men? There are days on which I have to acknowledge I will be the reverse of heroic; days on which I cannot perform. Funnily enough, I find that when I admit this, I begin to gather the strength to get on with the job.

Manly man's plight remains profound. He cannot ask a woman what has gone wrong with him because you don't confide in subordinates. And in any case there is no guarantee that women are still prepared to listen. Sisterhood is not only power-ful, it is a darn sight more interesting than ministering to men's wounded vanity. Neither can he confide in men-friends because their knee-jerk reflex would still be to put the boot in out of self-protection. In an age of transition, this is where the agony lies. Because men need women, they must attract them by being sympathetic and in order to qualify for sympathy, you have to make yourself vulnerable. Yet manly man has for centuries been acquiring and polishing his defences. How can he escape from this state of self-induced siege? Answer – by ideology. Mainly by means of the media. Mainly by men telling him in print or film that it's manly to be gentle, then showing him how.

I feel strongly that it is very unintelligent not to understand your own emotional life. The reason why women run rings round men is that men couldn't pass an O-level in describing their own feelings. That is why they often become violent – it is the only way we can convey our passions while somehow denying the importance of them.

Dr Joyce Brothers concludes:

'One thing is clear. Men are at a crossroads. They have headed our families, our governments, our businesses for centuries. They have explored our planet and the space around it. They have made our laws and fought our wars. But in less than the span of a lifetime, their authority is being eroded. They are no longer in secure command of the basic unit of civilisation, the family. The world they shaped is changing. One could think of them as sorcerers' apprentices who have triggered reactions they can no longer control. They can neither control them nor adjust to them.' (*What Every Woman Should Know About Men*, 1981).

If this were wholly true we would all be living hopeless lives unable to change the spellbound course of history. But men and mankind adapt or die, however suddenly their environment alters. I don't believe men can control the rebellion of women seeking liberty; nor should we try. So, since we've no wish to die, we'd better learn to adjust to it. This is in our own interests.

3 Nature or Nurture

'Whatever natural differences exist between men and women, they do not inevitably lead to social differences of the magnitude seen in most societies' (*New Society*, 12/5/1983)

'I think on the whole women are brighter than men, not academically particularly but in human terms. Perhaps it's biological but it doesn't matter why. Women are more reasonable. Men can be such stupid creatures at times. They are taught that it's manly to be aggressive. They are taught to be competitive at an early age by stupid grandparents who say: "See if you can run to the end of the room before Johnny". Seeing little children at each other's throats is the beginning of the end of civilisation' (Actor Tom Conti, *TV Times*, 16/10/1980)

'Women have more imagination than men – they need it to tell us how wonderful we are' (Arnold H., Glasgow)

In the two preceding chapters, I explored the idea that there exists a contemporary male crisis in human relationships. For evidence, I looked particularly at the rate at which men are currently succumbing to illness, stress and divorce, and as the common factor responsible for much of this destructive lifestyle, pinpointed men's inability to admit their limitations. I extrapolated from current trends to suggest that the traditional view of man as fighter, worker and family boss was in contradiction with social needs. In later chapters, I shall examine the details of men's difficulties at work and in the home, as fathers and lovers, but here I intend to look closely at the origin of the problem in childhood: how boys learn to differ from girls by becoming 'masculine'.

It only takes the first nine years of a boy's life to teach him the art of 'nonspeak'; to socialise him into a person who prefers *doing* to *being*. By that age, he is quite different from his girl contemporaries. They possess lively skills of introducing themselves, asking personal questions, revealing their own motives, sharing anxieties, airing problems. Generally speaking, a boy does not. While he is versatile with his hands at making things, he is embarrassed and timid when it comes to personal encounters and fairly incompetent when it comes to facilitating relationships.

This acquired sexual difference seems to be confirmed by experiments at the University of Denver, Colorado. Twenty pairs of nine-year-old boys were observed by psychologists through a one-way mirror as, two by two, they entered what appeared to be a large waiting-room. Once inside, each pair was told each other's first names and given 20 minutes to play together. Amongst other toys, a battered box of Lego bricks was made available as the play object.

In practically every case, the boys ignored each other as *people*. They displayed no personal curiosity. They didn't look into each other's faces. They didn't ask personal questions. They didn't volunteer information about themselves. Conversation was confined to the technical problems of Lego-design. In every essential respect, the boys stayed solitary and played by themselves.

The experimenters then moved on to test 20 pairs of nine-year-old girls. This time the results produced an equivalent bias in the opposite direction. The girls seemed to be everything the boys were not. They employed the Lego merely as a 'fidget-object' while they got down to the really interesting business of finding out about each other. They described where they lived, what their school was like, what they feared about different teachers, how it felt to be teased about wearing a tooth-brace, what they planned to do with the rest of the school holidays and whether they might aspire to a future college career. Frequently, they exchanged useful information about etiquette and they gave one another advice. By and large, they showed high levels of personal curiosity about each other which they were good at satisfying.

Thereafter the psychologists saw a whole series of children of both sexes with similar results; on all tests, *the girls revealed over three times as much about themselves to a stranger of the same sex as did the boys*. For the boys, the play was the primary focus; for the girls, it was the players not the play that mattered most. After-wards, it was discovered that the girls liked each other more as a result of their greater efforts towards self-disclosure. The boys remained mutually indifferent.

Earlier in their lives, as I mentioned in Chapter 2, it would not have been so. Little boys are just as affectionate, anxious and communicative as little girls. Up to the age of three, they are mother-focused, good at sharing feelings and fears. From three to six, however, they attempt to identify with their fathers and, as I will show in detail in Chapter 8, this may be where things start to go wrong. If, as US research has revealed, fathers only spend an average of 12 minutes per day with their children, it would not be surprising if boys did begin to lose their intimacy skills at this point.

Those who accept the traditional male stereotype of course, see muteness as a sign of masculinity. In Britain, it is manly in some classes to acquire a stiff upper lip. In America, the *macho* hero is tight-lipped like John Wayne, he tells you to button your lip like Steve McQueen or he never opens his lips, like Clint Eastwood. Since such people associate masculinity with male-ness they automatically accept that boys *naturally* keep them-selves to themselves. But can we really indict biology for what is the apparent absence of a skill of civilisation in nine-year-old boys? Let us examine the facts of human conception to see whether such gender differences are wholly a product of nature.

As you may recall from dark days in school, a human embryo contains 46 chromosomes. Each parent supplies 23 of these which then pair off. Sex is determined by only one of these pairs. Girls are designated 'XX', receiving the same chromosome from each parent, while boys are 'XY', their 'Y' chromosome coming from the father. The 'X' chromosome is much larger than the 'Y' and carries more programming information, but this chromosomal difference only seems to result in two major distinctions between the sexes. One is that, as noted in Chapter 1, men are more susceptible to stress and disease than women because their Y chromosome does not give them the protection women receive from their second X.

The second difference concerns a mental ability. Men seem to possess roughly twice as much 'visual-spatial ability' as women (O'Connor, *Structural Visualisation*, 1943). However, this does nothing to account for male taciturnity. Nor, as Tavris and Offir point out, does it mean that women are invariably bad at spatial tasks:

'The 25 per cent of them who have good ability do as well as the 50 per cent of men who have good ability (and better than the 50 per cent of men who do not)' (*The Longest War: Sex Differences in Perspective*, 1977).

Apart from this ability to identify embedded figures, no one has yet been able to show a direct connection between a specific gene and the range of alleged psychological or personality differences between the sexes.

If not the genes, could we suggest that prenatal sex hormones (a sort of biological traffic police) are responsible for closing men off from their gentler emotions? To many biologists, this has seemed a better bet. Until an embryo is six weeks old, there is no way of telling whether it will become male or female without examining the cell chromosomes. Before then, it contains tissue with the potential to develop *either* male *or* female external genitals. The genes decide whether to produce male or female *internal* sex organs and it is the hormones produced by these organs which 'sex' the brain and fashion penis or vagina. What is most interesting is that if the testes cannot produce male sex hormone (testosterone), the result is not a neuter but a being with male chromosomes and female genitals since:

'In the beginning, we are all headed towards femaleness . . . You can think of maleness as a type of birth defect' (Dr Stephen Wachtel, Memorial Sloan-Kettering Cancer Center, New York).

A popular theory suggests that it is this bathing of the brain in male sex hormones which results in men's 'aggressive-masculine' responses in life in place of 'passive-feminine' ones. This theory has been contradicted by the famous case study of a male identical twin whose penis was accidentally burned away at the age of seven months. His parents then had him sexually 're-assigned' and brought up as a little girl (Dr John Money *et al.*, *Man and Woman, Boy and Girl*, 1972), and by the age of four and a half, this little 'girl' had been so far socialised into the female role that she was in every respect a 'sister' to her former identical twin brother. This is despite the presumed effects of testosterone and its aggression-causing properties on 'her' brain at 42 days old. The impact of pre-natal hormones, therefore, cannot give us a complete account of the relative loss of inter-personal skills by nine-year-old boys. As traffic policemen, hormones are really only recommending a particular driving style, not actually writing a ticket.

In their vast review of the literature of sex differences (*The Psychology of Sex Differences*, 1974), Maccoby and Jacklin argue that males are indeed disposed *in general* to greater aggression (fighting, rough-and-tumble-play and threat behaviour) than females as a result of hormonal influences, but that this 'aggression' cannot be written into the definition of *all* masculinity nor be made an inherent quality of a *recommended* social role.

Ann Oakley (*Sex, Gender and Society*, 1972) concurs, pointing out that:

'. . . the differences between the sexes . . . are not as great as the differences *within* each sex'.

She implies that the differences in levels of aggression between males and females, for example, are not as great as the differences in levels of aggression between violent and pacific males. And when Doering *et al.* (*Sex Differences in Behaviour*, 1974) carried out a set of human experiments to examine, amongst other things, the correlation between high testosterone levels and hostility, they had to conclude that the results were 'not statistically significant'.

There is one other apparent biological difference between the abilities of men and women. Brain studies indicate that women tend to possess greater verbal ability than males because of the rate at which their brains develop with regard to the parts coping with language. Yet no one has suggested (least of all men) that women should take all jobs as writers, broadcasters, psychiatrists, politicians, salespeople, editors and publishers. Maccoby and Jacklin conclude that—apart from the characteristics discussed here—most of the other factors claimed in our cultural ideology to distinguish men from women have *never been demonstrated in properly conducted studies*.

This is also the opinion of Dr Hugh Fairweather (author of *Cognition*, 1976 and *Divided Visual Field Studies of Cerebral Organisation*, 1982). In a personal letter (16/6/1983) he told me that, in his view, there were no sex differences that were not either trivial or still a matter for controversy:

'*Verbal skills.*   Sex differences in language acquisition rates are trivial. This has been known for a long time but, such is the stereotype, has yet to penetrate the public mind. (Indeed, part of the reason it remains is just that: boys tend to appear in language-backward groups merely because they are expected to be language backward by their teachers: girls with similar disabilities "simply do not get referred.")

Brain differences (the view that females have two "left" verbal brain hemispheres). The data come from two sources: one, the relative abilities of the two normal hemispheres to deal with different kinds of information; and, two, the effect of damage restricted to one or the other hemisphere. Females are supposed to have their abilities more symmetrically represented, and hence to be less affected by damage to either half-brain (males are, as it were, held to have all their cognitive eggs in one hemisphere, and thus to be more susceptible). This view is quite simply unsupported in the literature. There is, in sum, little reason to suppose that male and female brains are any differently organised at all'.

Perhaps then we should turn to our environment for an explanation of gender differences. From birth to puberty and beyond, there is no doubt at all that males and females are subjected to different educations by parents and schools. There is a huge mass of evidence which describes the endorsement males are given to show their assertiveness while girls are taught passivity. Male babies soon after birth are awake more often than females, they move more and make more facial expressions (Phillips, King and Dubois, *Journal of Child Development*, September 1978). This would obviously seem to be one of the effects of prenatal hormones. But thereafter, since parents still feel biological sex implies different gender roles, newborn babies are subject to discriminatory treatment. For example, as we noted in the last chapter, mothers exercise boys' limbs more. At seven weeks old, parents speak more 'sweetly' to girls than boys. Over a third of first-time mothers studied by psychologist Anne Oakley said they thought their relationship with their baby was decisively affected by its sex. By the age of three, children already know to which sex they belong. In America, by the age of four, children have watched over 3000 hours of television giving ample opportunity to imbibe the message that men are tough guys and women use excessive quantities of shampoo in order to look pretty. By the age of seven, the interests and occupations of boys and girls are noticeably different, while by the time they've reached the age of 9–11, these activities have 'polarised sharply' (Newson and Newson, *The Sex-Role System*, 1978).

It is now well established that parents have a sex-role 'stereotype' to which they expect their child to conform; or rather, if he or she does not conform, they don't feel at all comfortable about it. Thus the Newsons also found that parents generally expected boys to be little rascals and girls to be little angels. We shall see in Chapter 4 just what happens in adult relationships intended to be equal partnerships when the psychological impact of this double standard strikes home. Contradictory messages merely produce contradictions:

'Before marriage, boys will be boys and girls will be virgins. After marriage, boys will be boys and girls will be faithful',

and so on into divorce.

Thus social pressure is firmly applied to *both* sexes from birth. Whatever the natural tendency of males to be active, this is soon superseded by parental direction to be downright assertive. On top of an inherited potential to be over-active, society imposes stern standards of male superiority. Feminists around the world have been quick to notice this since the 1870s. But what hasn't been given previous prominence is the price men have to pay, emotionally, physically and sexually, for being expected to achieve more than the opposite sex in work and play, while still competing with as many of their own biological peers as will take up the challenge. The loss of intimacy skills by the age of nine is only part of the story.

In early puberty, erotic differences between the sexes become even more marked:

'The adolescent boy has his eroticism imposed by nature. There is an enormous rise in the erotogenic hormone testosterone, which can produce intense sexual interest when administered . . . Nocturnal orgasms occur . . . In contrast, the girl experiences a rise in the female hormones oestrogen and progesterone. These contribute little to her eroticism and may even detract from it . . .' (Dr Alayne Yates, *Sex Without Shame*, 1979).

The male androgen levels rise, the young man is primed to reach

'The stereotype decreeing that, say, prodding the insides of cars is a "male" activity and sewing a "female" one has an obvious implication. Males and females may be brought up to do different types of things and, as a result, become competent in different spheres. But a stunningly simple experiment has just shown that males and females may only have to *think* that a task will be better performed by the opposite sex to do badly at it.

As a result of research by Dilys Davies at London University Institute of Education, David Hargreaves – who is lecturer in psychology at Leicester University – decided to ask children to play with a "wiggly wire". This is the game you often find at school fetes – you have to pass a wire loop all the way down a wiggly wire without touching it. If you do brush against it, a bell rings.

Hargreaves got 38 boys and 44 girls aged between ten and eleven to try this manual steadiness task. But he told half the children. "This is a test to see how good you would be at mechanics or operating machinery," and the other half, that it would test "how good you would be at needlework – sewing and knitting".

Compared to the number of errors the children made when they were given instructions "appropriate" for their sex, both boys and girls did significantly worse on the task if they thought the game tested a skill that was the "prerogative" of the opposite sex. "So apparent sex differences in certain abilities," Hargreaves says, "may be even less ingrained than people might think." (*New Society*, 10/3/1983).

orgasms, society sanctions his re-charged sexuality but not in a specifically healthy fashion. By his parents he is encouraged far more than his sisters to express his sexiness but masturbation is frowned on, petting is joked about and marriage (to a less experienced 'inferior') is quite quickly promoted as the safest haven for the restless libido.

But by his peers he is under pressure to perform. He is not biologically forced to be rampant, but he is socially expected to operate his sex-life as a primary source of identity, power and prestige. This idea of competition increases the pressure, not only on his virility, but on his entire personality. The price of failure is high; the risks in 'letting go' or displaying emotion get higher still; his sex-drive can become fenced in, protected, channelled into safe outlets or sublimated altogether into other prestige projects. He may even start to feel fear in the presence of those he desires. On this note, we can begin to re-evaluate some of those supposed differences between the sexualities of the sexes.

Are men *emotionally* frigid? In Anglo-Saxon countries, it is females who are considered passionate, scatter-brained and irrational; in Iran, on the contrary, it is men who are credited with excitability and women who are assumed to be level-headed:

> 'Similarly, if someone tells you that men tend to be unemotional and insensitive, it may be because he or she has ignored situations that allow men to be expressive' (Tavris and Offir, 1977).

When it comes down to a question of the goo-ing and gurgling 'ecstasy-response' to small furry animals, Phyllis Berman (*Attraction to Infants* . . ., 1975) certainly found that men were just as likely as women to feel it. They just tended to suppress it, that's all, particularly in public.

Are men more promiscuous than women? In a *cultural* sense yes, since there has always been that double sexual standard encouraging men to scatter wild oats and women to store them, and this has always been bolstered, as far as women are concerned, by religious teaching. If you look at 'dating behaviour' in Boston, as Anne Peplau and colleagues did ('Sexual Interaction in Dating Relationships', *Journal of Social Issues*, Volume 33, 1977), you can arrive at figures which show that:

> 27% of courted Roman Catholic women were able to resist intercourse
> > *compared to*
> 16% of Jewish women
> > *and a mere*
> 2% of Protestant women.

But religious affiliations had no impact whatsoever on the 'resistance' levels of men. In a further support of the thesis, male homosexuals are said to be 'notoriously' more promiscuous than women of either inclination, gay or straight, but this may be because of the particular pressures within this social group to prove their 'gay manhood'.

Surely it is a note of evolutionary caution which, in the past, has played a major part in preventing women from indulging in numerous, random sexual encounters. Before the advent of efficient contraception, a woman had to 'save herself' for the most suitable mate, both biologically and socially, since whoever she chose would put her out of circulation for nine months of pregnancy followed by 16 years of child-rearing. Sex for her *had* to mean a long-term relationship. Now in the age of the oestrogen pill this consideration need no longer concern her and it is social mores which play the major part in governing her sexual behaviour. Many men still consider a woman who 'sleeps around' a slut.

It may still be true that subconsciously women (and even men) seek an ideal breeding partner when considering potential liaisons, but since many couples consciously choose not to have children nowadays this cannot be the full story.

At present, men certainly are still more sexually active than women by all the obvious statistical measures: numbers of partners, frequency of orgasm, homosexual encounters, sexual fantasies, masturbation and fetish behaviour. All surveys on the subject since Kinsey agree that adolescent boys, for example, masturbate more than adolescent girls; this contrasts with the situation soon after birth when both sexes masturbate with equal regularity. Multiple climaxes for both sexes have been recorded during the very first year of life. The frequency of female sex play, however, declines rapidly with the early school years until the time of puberty when its renewed rate of increase is still far outstripped by that of males.

But this overall picture is beginning to change. We now realise that male and female patterns of sexuality are also differently timed. Women reach their biological peak for sexual response at or around the age of 40; men are past their peak by the age of 20. The availability of contraception and a new female self-assertiveness have undoubtedly helped many women to increase their 'rate of promiscuity' if we set no higher value to it than that. Most surveys indicate new levels of pre-marital sex for both sexes so that even the Mother's Union of Great Britain has come to regard the experience as normal (Ruth Hook, *Choosing Marriage*, 1978). Sex is a learned behaviour and if society doesn't teach it the individual won't acquire it. Those who argue seriously that men will always be more sexually active than women are overlooking the fact that we have only known how the human female sexual system works in any detail for less than 20 years, since the publication of *Human Sexual Response* by Masters and Johnson in 1966. How women's sexual behaviour will develop as a result of this knowledge remains to be seen.

It is still too early to tell whether men and women's different sexual behaviour is a result of biological facts or social pressures. But it is clear that the subject is related to the wider one of the interaction of men and women in society in general. The 'droits des seigneurs' of specially promiscuous males are logically bound up with general dominance by males. The right to sex with many partners is really a perk of office, as female senior management may one day discover. Ethologists argue that the pecking order in animal species is reproduced in human societies with males in command and the strongest males bossing the remainder as in a stag hierarchy.

At its lowest interpretation, men today stick to traditional role definitions in their own self-interest since they don't want to do housework:

'I've been married to a Fascist and married to a Marxist and neither one of them took out the garbage' (complaint attributed to a well-known actress).

But there is more to it than that. Men have always taken great pains to avoid any work so defined as women's work, whether this has consisted of sowing and reaping *or* housework. A balanced division of labour makes a great deal of common sense, but men conveniently ignore this. They have pretty universally held women's work in dis-esteem, whatever it is. Since many Soviet doctors are female, for example, the status of Russian doctors is quite low when compared to that of their Western counterparts. But we still haven't really explained why men should need to feel like this – or even why they dominated in the first place.

Redgrove and Shuttle (*The Wise Wound*, 1978) suggest that exclusion from the 'magic' of menstrual rhythms and childbirth contributed in men to a grave sense of timorous inferiority despite their physical predominance. This psychological anxiety led them to the compensatory illusion that hunting was more 'significant' than nurturance and that the deliverers of protein should enjoy a higher status than the deliverers of children. Many psychological theories are built on the premise that men are afraid of women since women can do what men can never do: i.e. give birth. Hence it is easy to suggest that men acquired their initial dominance (enough to teach them ruling ways) through the negative face of biology. Since they couldn't be *re-producers* so they became food *providers* accumulating in this process sufficient extra 'hunting-strength' to direct and rule the roost.

This theory is, of course, by no means widely accepted. Steven Goldberg (*The Inevitability of Patriarchy*, 1977) argues that male dominance is inevitable because:

'The neuroendocrinological differences between men and women engender different male and female behaviour . . . and . . . these differences set limits on, and give direction to . . . social institutions'.

But if this is so, that men have innate tendencies to dominance, why are they currently losing them? Equal rights legislation is being passed by men in most of the world's civilised countries. If Goldberg's theory is to hold water, it must hold water in both directions.

One direction in which the views of nearly all the biological determinists such as Goldberg seem to leak is in their attempt to define that behaviour which they regard as exclusively 'masculine'. You can usually test the hole in this by looking at their account of homosexuality.

Glenn Wilson and David Nias (*Love's Mysteries*, 1976) are a case in point. They incline towards the 'sex hormone' explanation of homophilia. Briefly, they envisage that a percentage of male babies is homosexually programmed for life just prior to birth when the foetal brain is deprived of its rightful exposure to the male sex hormone testosterone, or bathed in an inappropriate dosage of the female sex hormones oestrogen and progesterone. As a result, the brain is not 'triggered' to produce a 'masculine' disposition. Instead, the male's behaviour remains 'unaggressive, inward-looking, arrested'. Then, at puberty, his 'feminised' brain does not stimulate the testicles to produce testosterone in sufficient quantities, so his behaviour remains permanently 'unaggressive, inward-looking, arrested'.

Yet, quite apart from the argument concerning whether male hormones do *cause* 'male' behaviour (which has yet to be proved), what yardstick of behaviour have Wilson and Nias used against which to measure homosexual behaviour? If being inward-looking and peaceful are attitudes of mind which are not only accepted in heterosexual men, but also admired, then homosexual behaviour does fall within the *range of male behaviour*. All you are left with then are two groups of perfectly 'masculine' men, one preferring the same sex and one preferring the opposite sex (although you still don't know why). Wilson and Nias appear to believe that homosexuality in men is by definition a non-masculine behaviour; but that is to read your conclusions into your premises with a vengeance.

What seems to have escaped all the great psycho-biologists is a truth which Juliet Mitchell captured in her review of literature on men and manhood (*New Society*, 12/6/1980):

> 'The point is that *masculinity and femininity only exist by virtue of their difference from one another* . . . [in our present crisis], there is a temptation to search for definitions of being-women or being-men as though these states could exist as meanings independently of one another . . . Locating the difference within each discrete entity misses the point that difference is only a mark of a relationship between two terms. Contrast men and women with giraffes and men and women become the same.
>
> But, as of now, for human society to exist at all, men and women must be marked as different from each other. It is the social meaning of the mark and not the discovery of a so-called "real difference" (be it within culture or biology) that must be the starting point for examining the significance of the human distinction between the sexes'.

From this we can learn two things. The first is that we may have a great deal more freedom as men and women than we thought to develop our own style or pattern of life. The arrival of theories of *self*-determination is a little like General Blücher turning up on the field of Waterloo: just in time to save the world from imperious chauvinism. Coupled with the provision of reliable tools of social engineering (above all the contraceptive pill), this can enable the relatively affluent Westerners of today to make their own beds and lie on them. The second is that, even though masculinity and femininity only exist by virtue of their difference from each other, that difference does not place them at *opposite* ends of a single continuum: many people are both masculine *and* feminine.

This is the view of psychologist Sandra Bem who has applied the term 'psychological androgyny' to those who show both characteristics strongly. She has also asserted that the people who see themselves as masculine and feminine to equal degrees are the psychologically healthy ones, not those who are strongly sex-typed. (To find out how androgynous you are, see p. 38.) Several experiments have found that androgynous people scored higher on questionnaires measuring psychological adaptability, self-esteem, social competence and ability to cope with stress. On the other hand, those stereotyped as exclusively 'masculine' or 'feminine' are people who over-rely on the culture's definitions of maleness and femaleness to structure nearly all their perceptions of the world and to re-inforce their own behaviour and self-image. They seem to need others to do their thinking for them. Cultural conservatives will regard with horror the fact that:

> 'A woman has just come top of a course training young army officers in battlefield skills such as laying minefields, erecting bridges across rivers and demolition work ... Men came to the course after about seven months at Sandhurst; [but] Lieutenant (Jan) Harper had only nine weeks' basic training with the Women's Royal Army Corps ... She had [prior] technical knowledge, being the only member among the 21 on the course who was a graduate civil engineer.' (*Times*, 1/8/1983).

Those men who feel particularly threatened by such news – of a sort which is daily getting more commonplace – should reflect that as long ago as 1905, when Freud published his famous *Three Essays On Sexuality*, it was affirmed that the sexes do not belong in bio-cultural ghettos:

> 'Every individual ... displays a mixture of the characteristic traits belonging to his own and to the opposite sex'.

It is often noted that each sex contains the hormones of the other and we do, without doubt, originate in the same species. C. G. Jung extended the idea of human completeness to mean that no man should consider himself whole unless his male 'half' (his *animus*) naturally dovetailed with his female 'half' (his *anima*). This yields the paradox that in one vital respect to be 'masculine' includes the predicate of being 'half feminine'. I take this to mean being able to imagine sympathetically what it must be like

How Androgynous are You? (after Bem: *Journal of Consulting and Clinical Psychology*, 42, 155–162)

Decide on a scale of 1–7 how accurately each of the following descriptions can be applied to you. If you plump for 1 it means the word or phrase is never or almost never true while a 7 means that it is always or almost always true.

1	self-reliant	23	sympathetic
2	yielding	24	jealous
3	helpful	25	has leadership qualities
4	defends own beliefs	26	sensitive to others' needs
5	cheerful	27	truthful
6	moody	28	willing to take risks
7	independent	29	understanding
8	shy	30	secretive
9	conscientious	31	makes decisions easily
10	athletic	32	compassionate
11	affectionate	33	sincere
12	theatrical	34	self-sufficient
13	assertive	35	eager to soothe hurt feelings
14	flatterable	36	conceited
15	happy	37	dominant
16	strong personality	38	soft spoken
17	loyal	39	likeable
18	unpredictable	40	masculine
19	forceful	41	warm
20	feminine	42	solemn
21	reliable	43	willing to take a stand
22	analytical		

to see and feel the world from a woman's point of view as well as your own. (Very often, the overly masculine male is, of course, repudiating his own female component when dismissing women as inferiors.)

Even so, being male *is* different from being female. The bodies and their functions *are* different. The experiences inside them must be different at different ages. Men, on the whole, have fewer bodily reminders of their maleness than women have of their femaleness. Adult men don't seem to have hormone cycles of any great significance whereas women are governed by the 'wise wound' of monthly menstruation which, as Redgrove and Shuttle have shown, is far more than a tide of reproductive

44	tender	53	does not use harsh
45	friendly		language
46	aggressive	54	unsystematic
47	gullible	55	competitive
48	inefficient	56	loves children
49	acts as a leader	57	tactful
50	childlike	58	ambitious
51	adaptable	59	gentle
52	individualistic	60	conventional

Scoring

a) Add up your ratings for items 2, 5, 8, 11, 14, 17, 20, 23, 26, 29, 32, 35, 38, 41, 44, 47, 50, 53, 56. and 59, and divide the sum by 20. This is your Femininity score.

b) Add up your ratings for items 1, 4, 7, 10, 13, 16, 19, 22, 25, 28, 31, 34, 37, 40, 43, 46, 49, 52, 55, and 58, and divide the sum by 20. This is your Masculinity score.

c) Subtract your Masculinity score from your Femininity score, and multiply the result by 2.322. If the result is greater than 2.025, you are sex-typed in the feminine direction. If it is smaller than −2.025, you are sex-typed in the masculine direction. Bem considers a score between 1 and 2.025 to be 'near feminine' and a score between −2.025 and −1 to be 'near masculine'. A score between −1 and 1 means you are not sex-typed in either direction; you are androgynous.

Footnote: the Bem test obviously relies on traditional stereotypes within its formula.

tension; it supplies and regulates female libido and creativity. Men do not feel this tie to earth and moon and natural rhythms and may have to manufacture routines for themselves. They are more liable to get out of touch with the human scale. The central function of reproducing offspring is denied to them, whatever significance we care to read into this. They have no menopause.

Even if all the stereotypes about men and women were proved to be false, girls and women would still see the world differently from boys and men. They think of themselves as different, they make different plans and have different histories, and this sets the stage for a self-fulfilling prophecy:

'. . . because when people think they are different, then in some sense they really are' (Tavris and Offir, 1977).

Our difficulty is to avoid regarding these cultural clues as programming cues. It is impossible to disentangle completely the 'real' differences between men and women from the socially imposed ones. But it is perfectly possible to conclude that they are not great enough to lead inevitably to the social distinctions between the sexes seen in most societies today. As John Stuart Mill protested even in 1869:

'I deny that anyone knows or can know the nature of the two sexes as long as they have only been seen in their present relation to one another' (*The Subjection of Women*).

4 Men with Women: Nonspeak

'Each of us possesses, in his heart, a royal chamber. I have bricked mine up . . .' (Flaubert)

'He, of course, is too busy to notice all the details of our relationship' (Sonia, wife of Leo Tolstoy)

'Steph works non-stop about the house doing all those housewife's chores that men come to expect as the norm. I only have to put a tee-shirt in for washing one day and it's cleaned, ironed and back on the shelf by noon the next day' (ex-motor cycle racing champion, Barry Sheene, writing about his live-in girlfriend, in *Leader of the Pack*, Barry Sheene, 1983)

'In a marriage it is all very well to say two are made one. The vital question is "Which one?"' (Anon.)

The traditional model of marriage is alive, but not well, and living, amongst other places, in West London. One of my clients came to see me because her husband's behaviour had grown intolerable. Except for the shouting, she thought the marriage was over. As a wife she felt she couldn't take any more and as a self-respecting human being she didn't see why she should. Twenty-three years of loving the same man was about to stop. When she had got some of this off her chest, I asked her what he'd done that was so wrong?

'That's just it,' she said, 'it's not what he does, it's what he doesn't do. He's a marvellous provider. He gets up at six and is out of the house by seven and I don't see him again until eight at night. He's a plumber with his own company

on Local Government contract work and his time is
booked up for the next five years. I work as well and I also
do his book-keeping for him. We have two children, a
caravan in Sussex and everything material in the world.

But when he comes in I could tell you what he will do
every single day of his life. He'll open the door, kiss me on
the cheek, ask me if my day was OK, make a cup of tea, sit
in the chair *and tune out*.

He can stay like that for the rest of the evening. The kids
could start World Wars III, IV and V and he wouldn't
notice. He'll probably put the television on and sleep
through the programme till closedown.

Come bedtime, he'll try on a kiss and a cuddle and if I
seem in the mood he can make fantastic love. We've always
been good together that way. But if I don't respond at once
he'll flop back on his side and snore. And these days I'm
so angry I don't feel like it very much at all. I've told him
things have got to change but he just stands there and
looks silly saying "What on earth do you want me to
do?".

How do I tell him I want him to, like, *be there?*'

It transpired that this woman was not asking for the moon, even
though the present state of affairs was bad enough to make her
think about getting a divorce. It was certainly true that she would
like her partner to give her an extra segment of his time. But the
only significant change she was seeking concerned the nature of
his behaviour during shared personal moments. She wanted his
attention. She wanted him to concentrate as hard on her as he
evidently found no difficulty in doing on his work. She wanted to
be wooed. She wanted to be entertained. She wanted to hear
about his feelings. *She wanted him to be her friend.* And in return,
she was prepared to look after the identical needs in him as she
has done *without being asked* for the previous 23 years. They are
called *mature dependency needs*, culminating in the desire for
adult *intimacy*, which is the subject of this chapter.

Time was, of course, when intimacy was thought only to occur
in the columns of the *News of the World* as a curiously inept
euphemism for copulation:

'And then Trooper Wintergreen and Mrs Marsden were
intimate in the conservatory. I made my excuses and
left . . .'

In the latter part of the twentieth century, however, intimacy is rapidly acquiring the trappings and status of a 'buzz' word. Intimacy is what women now require from men alongside the lineaments of gratified desire. Men want the same thing only they don't know it or can't bring themselves to say it.

As we saw in Chapter 1, failure to generate intimacy is one of the primary causes of divorce. Sociologist Dr Robert Chester of the University of Hull is on record as saying that the 'intimate quality of a relationship is now the only factor in a preponderance of cases which decides whether or not a given marriage will continue'. Almost one in three new UK marriages will end in divorce. Five years ago, the figure was one in four. Twelve years ago it was one in 10. In the remaining years of this century between five and six million adults in this country will become involved in divorce. There has been a crucial change in the nature of marriage. What was formerly a partnership of the male breadwinner and female housekeeper has turned into the union of free choice. People can now afford to do on their own those things such as child-raising and home-making which previously required a two-person economic alliance. So the question of a long-term partnership is now optional and the relationship tends to be abandoned if the intimacy is poor. The work of Robert Chester as well as that of Geoffrey Gorer (*Sex and Marriage in England Today* . . ., 1971) shows that failure to achieve emotional potential in marriage causes intolerable pain and it reveals that all classes see the issue from a similar perspective. Today, each group in society has high expectations of marital self-fulfilment, companionship and the sharing of confidences. (For more perspective on this subject, see my summary of facts and figures regarding marriage and divorce on page 44.)

It was not always so. In 1640, the expectation of life at birth in England and Wales was 32 years. The chance of a couple dying in their 20s and 30s was as great as it is today in one's 60s. Marriages were often impersonal affairs arranged by senior members of the two families concerned and the couple only had a limited refusal option. The death of a partner or indeed a child was such a frequent occurrence that people could be forgiven for not getting too romantically attached to their families and the actual duration of marriage was on many occasions no more than a few years. In London, in 1764, 49 per cent of all recorded children died by the age of two and 60 per cent by the age of five. In this sort of environment, the *personnel* of a marriage was far less important than the *functions* each partner performed. If you lost a

Marriage and divorce

In the 1960s, the *Futurist Magazine* predicted that marriage would be dead by 1990. It won't. Marriage is still as popular as ever and over 90 per cent of the adult population is nuptially tied. However, the ever-rising divorce rate and the trend towards cohabitation both pose important questions about the desired quality of marriage.

Modern divorce started in 1857.

It took nearly 100 years for the first million Britons to get divorced.

It took a further 15 years for the second million.

It took only six more years for the third million.

One in five men and women born in 1950 will have married for the second time by the age of 50. Currently, divorce runs at 150,000 cases annually affecting up to a million people, half of them children. In 1940, by contrast, there were just 6915 divorces.

1 Children and fathers

You can never divorce children. Nor is it desirable for the man to 'get out of their lives, to give them a clean break'. That's just you being selfish. You will always remain their father, whatever your changed relationship with their mother. Too many parents assume the 'kids will cope', but divorce always hurts children and they wish their parents wouldn't do it. The golden decision is always to estimate which is the more damaging hurt to inflict on them—a foul marriage or a foul divorce. Bear in mind that children often perceive a bad marriage as perfectly OK from their viewpoint and that they nearly always blame themselves for any subsequent breakdown. They need ongoing contact over the years with both parents to gain the necessary reassurance that this is not true.

2 Wives and husbands

There's a yawning credibility gap between what we expect a wedding to bring and what we get. Teenage marriages have always been most vulnerable to divorce but new evidence shows that the higher divorce rate during the past 10 years has even hit marriages thought least

husband or wife, you got a new one. If your children died, you sighed and set about producing some more. In a world of this kind, of course, divorce was superfluous. Nature did it for you.

By the nineteenth century, however, divorce had to be positively introduced for the masses (previously it had been confined to Henry VIII and those who could work a private Act of Parliament) in order to cope with the fact that by this time marriages lasted long enough for their 'quality' to begin to tell. Better sanitation and health care had increased everyone's life ex-

likely to break down. Even first marriages of those who marry at relatively older ages are now likely to suffer.

● Almost three in every five marriages in which the husband married as a teenage bachelor would be expected to end in divorce (more than a third before the 10th wedding anniversary).

● Half of all teenage brides who married as spinsters would be expected to divorce by the 30th wedding anniversary.

● Most divorces occur after five to nine years of marriage, so the seven-year itch is no myth. But marriages lasting 20+ years are almost equally at risk. These two categories account for 52 per cent of all divorces.

● Marriage between those aged over 25 at the wedding is now subject to a one in four divorce rate.

● The peak rate of re-marriage occurs in the age group 25–29.

● The divorce rate for those on their second marriage is already approaching 50 per cent.

● One-parent families now amount to 11 per cent of all families and include one and a half million children. The cost to the Exchequer in benefits and medical care was recently calculated by Dr Jack Dominian as at least £1 billion annually. A 1976 report suggests things may be even worse than we think. Perhaps the divorce figures reveal only *half* of all broken marriages, with people just living apart or, worse still, soldiering on through a minefield of hate. By far the biggest cost is to people's emotions.

3   Cohabitation

More young people are deferring marriage by choosing to cohabit. As many as 40 per cent in Sweden and 20 per cent in France have established 'living together' as a way of life. The UK figure is over 10 per cent and growing steadily.

pectancy while an emphasis on feelings generated by the Romantic Movement increased people's expectations of personal happiness. Unfortunately, the chosen institution – matrimony – regularly failed to deliver the goods.

Today, the Western world has reached a point where the duration of the 'Augustinian-style' marriage ('the permanent union of one man with one woman') is approaching an unprecedented 40-to-50-year cycle. Modern couples can even anticipate an unparalleled quarter of a century of proximity after their children have left home. It is therefore deeply significant that 25 per cent of divorces take place only after 20 years of apparently successful or, at least, tolerable alliance; and also that fidelity increasingly dissolves into adultery in the middle years. This search for variety indicates just how important intimacy is to successful relationships. Although sex itself is no guaranteed path to conjugal rapport, it is one means of finding it, keeping it or replacing it. This does not mean that a straying spouse necessarily breaks up the happy home. A high value is placed nowadays on closeness and shared feelings so that even adultery may be forgiven provided a husband and wife can sustain the intensely personal side of their marriage. For instance, in a recent *Sunday Times*' opinion poll on choosing a menu for a tolerable marriage (May 1982) 'fidelity on the part of the spouse' rated only 11th place, way behind 'being able to talk to your partner', 'having a good sexual relationship' and even 'financial security'. A mere 15 per cent of the sample insisted that sex outside marriage was always wrong. A virtue-laden Family Doctor booklet on marriage published in 1981 supported the view that:

'. . . an affair is *not* the occasion for bringing a marriage to an end. Most couples can live with such an event. Far more important is to discuss the reasons behind it and if possible repair it' (Dr Jack Dominian, *Marriage – Making or Breaking?*).

This includes being more open about the underlying feelings of lust, revenge, betrayal or guilt.

Staying with divorce for the moment, if outside affairs no longer make a marriage 'intolerable', why does the divorce rate keep on climbing up the graph paper? The answer seems to me to be that the biggest bar to intimacy between men and women is men and women – especially men. Unfortunately, men have great difficulties in accepting this:

'I noticed our marriage was getting a bit dodgy and I thought now we're going to Marriage Guidance, this will sort Jane out – because I was associating our problems with Jane, just Jane. She was getting over-tired and what have you – and consequently she had no time for me. But when we got there, after the first couple of sessions, it was beginning to dawn on me that it was 60 per cent my fault. I just wasn't taking any notice of her. She was becoming part of the furniture.' (Tony Crick, farmer, *Men . . .*, BBC2, 1984).

By the age of nine, a lot of little boys are already unable to relate to their fellows except through an activity. Personal speech has become alien to them. Beginning a sentence: 'I can see that you feel X about Y', which is the standard test of a good inter-personal communicator, would stick in their throats like a fish-bone. Psychologist Carol Gilligan theorises:

'Women feel vulnerable when they lose touch with relationships. The opposite is true for males. You see, this is the male fear of intimacy. There is not much personal intimacy among men. They turn to women for that.

Look at the great literature written by men about love. In men's writing great love ends in death: Romeo and Juliet, Tristan and Isolde, Anna Karenina. Men's fantasies connect closeness with death. Women on the other hand connect closeness with safety.' (*In A Different Voice: Psychological Theory and Women's Development*, 1982).

Recent research has confirmed these views, but it has also disturbed the traditional idea that men have little *need* of intimacy. Women may feel vulnerable when they lose touch with relationships, but they are the ones to call the whole thing off if they are not getting the right quality of emotional feedback:

'In several studies of courtship, cohabitation and close sexual partnerships, psychologist Elaine Hatfield has shown that women do indeed fall in love more slowly and carefully; however, they fall out of love more quickly. Men on the other hand, fall in love quickly and hang on desperately when love dies. This research indicates that men find it much more difficult to adjust to the loss of close relationships than traditionally supposed' (*Cosmopolitan*, May 1983).

In a study of courting couples in Boston, Massachusetts, it was found that the woman was responsible for 80 per cent of all break-ups, while an examination of the divorce statistics showed that wives were responsible for the legal initiation of about 75 per cent of American divorces.

The picture is the same in Britain. Men have apparently not

appreciated, says the *Daily Express* (February 1982) that modern women find it monumentally unrewarding to establish a close relationship with a tight-lipped Tower of Strength or similar edifice. Women want a man with inner qualities no less. It wouldn't be stretching the truth to suggest that women rate sympathy as their number one aphrodisiac. It certainly pushed something called 'sexual prowess' into seventh place in the *Express*. Add this to the *Sunday Times*' finding that only two per cent of men take any part in British housework to the everlasting despair of their womenfolk and you can begin to understand why for every man in Britain who divorces his wife, there *are* three women who divorce their husbands.

Two reasons help explain why this world-wide rejection is so hard for men to absorb. Firstly, they see their official relationships as being inextricably bound up with their status. This enhances their vulnerability, forcing them to be cagey about their true feelings lest they put these partnerships in jeopardy. Secondly, they really do possess dependency needs (whether they know it or not) and it's towards the satisfaction of these that their policy and diplomacy are for the most part directed. When the conversation reaches this point:

> She: 'Do you love me?'
> He: 'What is love?'

the man is usually attempting to provoke the woman into loving him 'for free', without him having to admit he wants to hear her say it, just as much as she wants him to declare for her. Dorothy Miell at Lancaster University has shown that men are:

> '. . . chronically resistant to disclosing their true feelings in relationships with females yet are very concerned to drive the female towards disclosing her own feelings, attitudes and beliefs. It is as if such behaviour is designed to give them strategic control over the relationship'.

The true purpose behind this drive for power over the woman is to compel her to make provision for the male's utter dependence on her by showering him with love and praise. The complication, of course, is that some of the drive and most of the needs are unconscious.

Men, if pushed, will give you their genuine opinion that they do *not* know what love really is. The field remains *terra incognita* and a veritable place of hidden terrors to boot. It stands to reason that if men are trained from soon after birth to control their feelings, even though the urge is present they will not have actually *felt* very much when desiring to hold, cuddle, cherish and surrender, especially in the presence of that inferior crew, women. And yet no man is the pirate island he likes to think himself and if he is not in receipt of routine 'loving strokes' then his 'spinal cord will shrivel up', as Dr Eric Berne has been considerate enough to remind him (*Games People Play*, 1964). Nowadays, women are exacting a price in reciprocity for providing men with the necessary love-strokes. They are even daring to insist that the male trick of romantic 'non-speak' would no longer fool a little girl of nine, let alone a woman:

> She: 'Do you love me?'
> He: 'What is love?'
> She: 'It means telling me you love me . . .'
> He: 'What if I don't?'
> She: 'Then tell me. I can take it.'

Schooled by the lack of communication in male dialogue, the feminist Juli Loesch has now alerted the world to its evasions by coining two new terms. One is 'testeria' – the inability to feel or express certain feelings. The second (an attempt to define the active phase of the first) is 'penisolescence' – the invasive effort to master one's own distress by mastering other people. Men, if not rattled, have been rumbled.

The best case we could make in our own defence has nothing to do with the alleged virtue of keeping a tight manly grip on personal feelings; we could with absolute justice point out that a great many women have not yet decided what it is they expect from men. Protection and provision? A lot of women still say yes. In the ring as a sparring partner? Ditto. By their sides as equals and mates? Yes. Beneath them as hen-pecked servitors? I'm afraid sometimes yes again.

If a modern Tarzan offers to look after a modern Jane she's almost as likely to be the type to take up the offer as the type who will karate-kick him in the unmentionables. As journalist Shirley Lowe was once so quick to emphasise:

> 'Even more confusing, these two Janes are frequently one and the same girl. The gentle homebody may well be a highly intelligent woman who resents being treated as a

bird brain with nothing on her mind but the price of beef, and all the toughest career girls I've ever met expected to be wooed and courted and sent flowers and pretty poems just like an old-fashioned frilly débutante' (*Over 21*, June 1977).

Ms Lowe (not a 'girl' herself I am sure) is kind enough to consider that one reason why men may be slow to betray their intimate moods is because they can have no idea what kind of reception they will get.

Nevertheless, the fact that the outside world is full of sophisticated confusion does not justify men's remaining mute. If women can start to make sense of the multiple psychological ambiguities of modern society (remember 'Women's Studies'?), then so too can men. I have always been impressed by what I call the 'parable of getting lost'. Whereas a woman will ask everyone for directions to her destination and get there, a man would rather stay lost than have to ask for outside help. It is the same in company as in the car. A man has a tongue in his head as well as a brain. He is at liberty to use both to discover what is going on. Have you ever listened to a good old bout of masculine un-talk?

'How's it going, Frank?'
'Fine, fine . . .'
'Business?'
'Never better . . .'
'And the operation?'
'Piece of cake . . .'

and a few weeks later you are astonished to hear that when Frank died from post-operative complications he was technically insolvent.

The only other justification for the traditional masculine reserve comes from an analysis of working class values as dictated by capitalistic demands. For in this case a man behaves in distant fashion within the home, as a patriarch and authority figure, in order to confirm his status as a worker, as the one who suffers in toil for the sake of his family. If he turned round and began helping domestically, he would devalue his efforts on the shop floor where what he does is 'man's work' from which he derives his identity. Home has to be seen as a haven of peace and quiet for the shattered man who brings home the bread. As I have already noted, this argument is dying a death from deindustrialisation. It will in future be increasingly difficult for such men to take their identity from their work when far fewer will have any. Nevertheless the attitude is at present still entrenched and often results in unhappiness:

> 'Working class marriages are less happy, partly because the husbands are often unsatisfactory confidants, and lead more independent social lives (like going to the pub and football). Some studies have found that unskilled workers have a more negative self-image. Their wives, on the other hand, feel perfectly adequate as wives and mothers. The fact that middle class couples spend more time with friends (who are shared) while working class people spend more time with their kin (who are not), may also be relevant' (Michael Argyle, 'What Makes Marriages Tick?', *New Society*, 12/5/1983).

There is quite a body of evidence to show that men are not particularly content within their traditional sex role in any case. One US survey showed that approximately 50 per cent of American women considered themselves to be happy, but less than a third of the men. It is curious that men should feel so bad when throughout historic times they have held social dominance.

Carol Gilligan believes we can discover a clue to male melancholy in the very distinctions of normal psychology. She claims that the 'official' model of human personal development is exclusively 'male-based'. Thus the authorised version of 'maturity' is seen as a matter of becoming 'autonomous and independent'. In her view this is overly partial to the male stereotype, since for women maturity might be seen as 'group autonomy', within a 'near-permanent network of inter-relationships in which the woman plays the central role'. She identifies with a cell of friends. She achieves an ethic of care rather than an ethic of detachment. She has an over-riding need to connect, which is why women describe themselves as wives and mothers even when they are also lawyers and doctors, unlike men's self-descriptions. And if dependent intimacy is a normal state of affairs for adult womanhood, could it not be the lack of this which makes some men lonely and unhappy? Could we go even further and suggest that men have got part of their basic printout of human psychology – male and female – wrong?

We certainly need some explanation to help us account for the widespread modification of traditional matrimony by both sexes.

If they are not in search of higher standards of intimacy, why are more couples at such pains today to test each other out in the routine of 'living together'? Is this not an attempt to enhance compatibility? To take less on trust than in the old marriage model since personal happiness is ultimately the only thing that matters? I would link this to all the information which stresses women's dislike of marital subservience, in particular the sort of survey which has shown that whereas 'in 1962, two thirds of US women agreed that the man takes the most important decisions in marriage, by 1977, two thirds of US women *disagreed* with the same proposition' (quoted by Brothers, *What Every Woman Should Know About Men*, 1982). I also read this as yet a further demand for intimate involvement on the part of the woman in all aspects of marital life, including knowledge of men's fears and concerns about finances, employment and the future.

Some men have been able to abdicate from the role of lordly patriarch entirely, if not always willingly. Two such were interviewed by journalist Veronica Groocock in the *Times* (6/5/1983), giving both an opportunity to explain that males are not compelled by any biological or cultural necessity to be bread-winners and decision-makers. John Tanner, a redundant professional, doesn't like what he calls his 'housewife's' job, but he makes an elegant fist of baking bread, cooking and cleaning. On the plus side, he sees more of his sons and has more control of the money, though there is less of it to spend. Richard Ambrose, on the other hand, an out-of-work trained electrician, has more happily adapted to being the 'house-husband':

'I can't see me getting a job anywhere, so this was the next best thing, because she's got opportunities (his wife is a residential social worker), you see, so why waste them? I'm a male version of my mother (she's a part-time cleaner in a dockyard). My mother was very houseproud. She was always cleaning: it was one of her fortes. In the same way, I'm inclined to get too involved with it. We have our little ups and downs in this. I'll say: "Get out of the way, I want to clean there."'

Does he mind having to ask Sue for money? 'Well, she never seemed to mind when she asked *me* for it!'

Sue chips in: 'It's not my money: it's ours' . . .

Richard: 'I can understand why a lot of marriages fail, 'cos they are two such *separate* people, poles apart, and the friction that causes. I don't consider myself totally *male*. I mean the mates that I would call *males* wouldn't know how to cook anything or even how to plug a vacuum cleaner in . . .'

As the structure of employment continues to change with increased leisure and increased redundancy, we are going to see more families like these where the keynote is the *interchange-ability* between the sexes of the roles of worker, domestic and nurturing parent. One welcome consequence of successful role-swapping is improved intimacy based on heightened awareness of the contribution previously made solely by the other partner. As John Tanner's wife, Sue, says:

'John is a lot more aware of what goes into running a house. Each of us appreciates the other one more than we did before'.

For her part, Sue Ambrose has always hated housework and could not be more appreciative of the burden her husband has, for the foreseeable future, lifted from her shoulders. And Sue Tanner has also learned how it feels to carry full responsibility as family wage-earner:

'I sometimes worry about what would happen if I lost my job. Every breadwinner does I suppose'.

Thus, in addition to improved intimacy, another very constructive by-product of some of the enforced task-sharing in British families is the realisation that the *skills* of intimacy can also be improved. Compatibility, in any case, is not just a question of chemistry. Most couples share love and commitment, says Dr Chester (University of Hull), but this by itself is not enough. They then have to find out how intimacy skills may be even further enhanced.

So, apart from swapping jobs, how do you learn to be intimate? Michael Argyle says:

'Several processes may contribute to the marital bond. Regularly taking part in activities which are satisfying and for which the other is necessary, makes the other partner valued. (This may be the male form of bonding.) Regularly talking, discussing personal problems, leads to a shared cognitive world. (Female friends talk a lot; perhaps this is the female form of bonding.) Satisfaction can be assessed from the balance of rewards and conflicts. In one study, for example, it was related to the amount of sexual intercourse minus the number of rows . . .' (*New Society*, 12/5/1983).

Of course, as Argyle was first to notice, enjoying a lot more sex and far fewer rows might well lead to divorce, because nothing has been said about the 'quality' of the sex and it is vital in any healthy relationship that there should be conflict as well as concord. A common complaint from women is that: 'You can't have a row with my bloke – he just walks away', which is, in fact, a denial of intimacy, albeit of the boisterous kind. This is because marriage, as Dr Chester explains, is a 'constant obstacle course'. There will be inevitable conflicts and these are necessary. Provided we can learn how to limit their destructiveness, they are good for us. The first rule, he says, is to listen. Some unpleasant conflicts cannot be evaded. The children, for instance, will rarely enhance your sense of contentment. They represent life stress. Because of their demands, you are often ready to go to sleep by the time your partner is ready to talk about a matter of importance or to make love. Therefore, says Chester, set up an appointment to listen and talk and to love. Take out time to feel the pulse, not just of your partner, but of the relationship as a whole. You can learn to pinpoint particular problem areas which perhaps always lead to hateful disputes.

You can increase rewards as well. Michael Argyle suggests having 'caring' days once a week, on which eight to 20 acts are carried out (giving flowers, a kiss, a compliment, a special meal). You can learn skills of negotiation:

'This includes training in contracts. In one contract, for example, the husband agreed to take the wife out two nights a week, while she agreed to sex games of his choice one night a week' (*New Society*, 12/5/1983).

This immediately reminds me of a couple who came for counselling (he, incidentally, was a psychiatrist) because the husband wanted to make love so frequently to his wife that she was getting switched off. We eventually arrived at a contract under which he could choose what they did on three nights of the week, she could choose on three nights and the last night was up for grabs. As a result, sex always took place on his nights of choice, it never took place on her nights of choice and it always took place on the night which was optional. Both were reasonably content with a compromise regulating marital sex to four times weekly.

Of equal importance to learning the art of sensible compromise is investing time and effort in 'bonding activities'. This means doing more things *together*, even if you end up down a pothole or panting in an aerobics class. Ideally, such activity should culminate in an important goal: a project to learn a useful skill such as cookery or carpentry is particularly suitable, but any shared interest is better than none. One couple I know remain perfectly content with their hobby of visiting the major supermarkets of the South of England by motor bike. Each to his own. Just remember there is no truth in the saying that people with nothing in common are the most compatible (that 'unlike poles attract'). In fact, their relationships tend to break up.

In general, being on your partner's wavelength is the path to successful intimacy, but it is also necessary to realise that the marital relationship is not an institution but a process. Unless you make a daily contribution to the partnership it will die. The self-exculpatory shout so often heard from the man: 'Well I married her, didn't I?' will cause no echoes. I'm afraid you have to marry her in spirit again and again till death do you part if you intend the union to be lifelong and stable.

You must go even further. In order to keep the partnership alive, you have to make a commitment to the relationship as a means of helping your partner grow and change. Contrary to the desires of many men, the act of bonding is not a method of keeping your wife exactly as she was, mentally and spiritually, on the day you married her. Since you are not required to stay the same, no more is she, and if marriage is used as an instrument to halt personal development, the predictable outcome is, again, divorce. When you reach the point of saying 'I can accept you as you are, please accept me', you have also accepted the psychological basis for growth through change, since the act of acceptance *is* an act of change. There is even a bitter-sweet comedy in some men's adjustment to this reality:

> 'A man stabbed by his wife when he returned home from a drinking bout told Inner London Crown Court last week: "I now have a great deal of respect for my wife, which I did not have previously"' (*Times*, 1/9/1983).

When men do accept that the power of the adult female should develop alongside their own, they will release women from endless mothering tasks on their behalf and themselves from a degrading domestic childishness. The more they manage this, the more true intimacy will grow, bringing them what they really wanted in the first place – stimulation, recognition, love.

Cases

The difficulty men have in articulating their feelings is a problem I often encounter in my work as a counsellor. Here are some case histories to illustrate how inadequate we men can be at relationships, and also some which show what can be achieved if you are prepared to put the old male values aside and form a 'partnership of equals'.

Jeanette: A marriage of nonspeak

'My husband is a good provider and father, the only two roles he takes seriously. When it comes to adults, he's a psychological blank, as bad with himself as me. When he's ill, he won't believe it. If things don't go his way, he shouts at them. When this doesn't produce results, he shouts louder. He never stops to think why ranting doesn't help. Presumably it always worked when he was a little boy and he's not about to change tactics in mid-stream.

'Needless to say he couldn't understand my need for peace and gentleness and so I fell in love with another man. When we started our affair, my husband was incapable of finding out about it. He had never noticed when I was depressed. He had no idea that he himself was overstressed. So how was he going to pick up on my moments of stolen joy? If anything, he began to enjoy life too, since I became more tolerant of his limitations, diverting my demands.'

Was Jeanette saying that men are gullible? 'In business, no. In the personnel department, definitely!' She thinks men generally like you to be literal. They like it even more if you can be literal in a large, cheerful voice. They positively adore it if your speech contains unimpeachable internal logic. And they'd vote you Wife of the Year if you turned into a beaming robot. 'What they cannot stand is emotional confrontation, when you start to fight, when you muddy the issue with feelings, when you take a rise out of them or when you begin to shout back. That's known as being irrational . . .'

Was Jeanette suggesting that women are more deceitful than men, so better able to get away with having an affair? 'Yes, because as the "undersex" we have had to evolve greater skills of manipulation and cunning.' Where men only see black and white in life, she says, women see many shades of grey. While men have principles, women have babies and so are forced to blend the rules of morality into those of personal survival. 'It's unsafe for women to be over-blatant, so we dissemble. We're good dissemblers since we understand ourselves. Generations of frustration, suppressed anger and jealousy amount to a crash-course in self-knowledge.'

Accordingly, Jeanette lied to her husband and made it stick. So, too, do thousands of other women who keep their affairs secret, sometimes for years. One wife plays golf for ten days every August in Spain but never unpacks her clubs. She claims that this 'marital holiday' lets her be an impeccable spouse for the rest of the year. Another woman plays the clarinet all over London with her husband's blessing, except that she can hardly assemble the instrument let alone blow a recognisable tune.

In general, such women are married to dispassionate, self-involved and work-centred men. Men who would rather receive than give, trained by their Mummies to inherit the earth and all that it contains. It is not really their fault that they would rather have married Mother than an equal but, alas, spoiled boys become emotionally deprived adults, which accounts for their extra-marital blinkers.

To many modern couples, Jeanette's marriage would seem dishonourable although both they and she are really seeking the identical goal of successful personal intimacy. Where she opts for quiet compromise within the system, however, others openly reject traditions which they believe hamper mutual solidarity.

John and Claire: An open marriage with legal force

Claire is 24 and John 48. He was formerly married to a writer and has two grown-up children whom he adores. After divorce, he lived with another woman for 11 years without being married. He did ask her but she said no.

Claire and John met five years ago when Claire turned up at John's work one day as a temp. She 'knew' in the first few hours that here was someone she was going to love and they got into bed the next day. Claire had previously had lots of sex relationships but she hadn't had a full love affair before. John had reached the platonic stage with his current lady without realising things were over. Claire knew she wanted to live with John. One year after John's other mistress left, Claire moved into John's house. They gave a party for family and friends in September last year to announce a joint 'commitment' but not yet a marriage. They work together in John's business but insist that work and home-life are kept separate.

'From the start', says John, 'it's been an Open Relationship. I see us as two individuals sharing our lives together rather than creating a joint life. We respect each other's freedom. If Claire makes love to another man or I make love to another woman it does *not* mean our relationship is on the rocks. I'd feel we were cheating *only* if the other didn't know.'

'I once found my previous lover in bed with another woman', says Claire. 'I just made a cup of tea for them both telling myself I'd cope with this situation much, much better by staying super-calm than by sticking a knife in him. It worked. I don't have sexual jealousy with John now. I'd think he was unfaithful if he spent Christmas with another woman. But he's always welcome to spend, say March 26th, with one.'

'Our ideas have worked for us', says John. 'We've got a good track record. But quite irrationally, for reasons she can't explain logically, Claire wishes to be legally married as far as the state is concerned.'

'I actually hate the idea', says Claire, 'that people are sniggering behind their hands: "Oh they're not *married*, you know, it's only temporary".'

'But Claire is not prepared to say and nor am I' says John, 'anything in the ceremony she doesn't mean, such as "we hold to this person exclusively" or "those whom God hath joined let no man put asunder".'

'Happily', he continues, 'we have found a branch of the Unitarian Chapel in Golders Green that offers a legal marriage ceremony where you can more or less write your own form of words including a sonnet by Shakespeare ("Let me not to the marriage of true minds admit impediment . . ."). The crucial words are we agree "to prefer each other's good" which in our case means having an open marriage as does the phrase later on in the service, "Two people secure to each other the enjoyment of their most personal needs . . .". We actually need outside love affairs. This is especially important in our case since when I'm 70 she'll be in her prime at 45 and her sex drive will probably be higher than mine (though I doubt it) and I would never want her to be unsatisfied.

'In business, the ambiguity of our present relationship creeps in. About a working wife I can be practical with colleagues and she stands on her own merits. But if we don't marry, the suggestion is always that I've got myself "a bit of fluff". I really don't think I should have to go through this but I accept marriage is a social matter which even concerns the milkman. Does he talk to the "Lady of the house" or what? If I say "consort" he asks me if I'm in the bloody royal family or something.'

'Yet we don't want to be thought of as "a couple",' says Claire. 'We think it's mad that the moment two people marry they are treated as a unit and two individuals with progressive lives come to a stop. Why do couples only socialise with couples or singles but never with *half* a couple? Married couples always seem to lose their friends.'

'Part of my love for Claire', says John, 'is to insist I don't diminish her freedoms. The payoff is of course I keep my own freedoms. I couldn't live with a possessive woman.'

'Our wedding is later this year', says Claire. 'I am choosing marriage, albeit an open one, because I think it will prevent ridicule but not imply joint ownership. For instance, although I love John dearly I am no longer "in love" with John. In fact, I happen to be in love with another man altogether but the vital point is I know it won't last . . .'

Michael and Chloë: Literary idealism and cohabitation

Michael Juvot and Chloë Theale live in Dorset. There's about 20 years difference in their ages but the partnership is equal and Michael does not play Big Daddy. Professionally, they are experts on 'women' – most of their recent books have concentrated on this subject. They have a child Flossie who has just started school.

'This is a blessing', says Michael, 'because now we can make love in the mornings again. I think regular, frequent sex is very important to a relationship. Preferably, we'd have sex daily, preferably in the mornings. Sex illuminates the day. It's not a thing for the night. It gives energy and creates trust between partners. If the woman is tired, specially from looking after children, she makes love differently. She's more passive. This affects the father. If the mother devotes her energy to the kids in the pre-school years, he gets jealous. It's the Joseph syndrome. He feels left out.

'I'm very keen on making love. One of the risks in our relationship was having the baby. Children alter the pattern of your free time. Before Flossie, we did a hell of a lot of screwing.

Now, we're just getting back into the swim. One famous Christmas, I remember, we made love 33 times in ten days holiday. Is that above average? I think it is.

'The future of marriage lies in not marrying. Lots of people shouldn't. You see, marriage is done' unconsciously. People don't think about it. They fall into it or get pushed in the deep end by their families. Living together, however, is conscious. People choose exactly how they wish to live; they set up the conditions in freedom. Marriage is to do with having property and kids. Living together is creative, it's to do with drawing out the personality and self-development.

'I think this difference is growing more distinct, especially to young people. They begin to realise they can either be sexual, loving, imaginative and creative. Or they can get married and buy their way of life ready-made.

'If a woman has a baby, she naturally becomes unconscious. She forgets things, she gets "pregnancy amnesia", she becomes placid and peaceful. The father falls into a parallel role. The institution of marriage is designed for such people. It supports those who can't be thinking for themselves. This is another reason why lots of people choose marriage when they choose to have children.

'When you marry, you also marry into a family. It's really a marriage of families. A woman needs her mother to tell her (by supporting her) that she is doing the right thing in having babies with this man. So she copies her mother's marriage.

'Basically marriage grew out of the need religion had to create more souls for God. That is why so many churches are opposed to contraception, abortion and permissiveness – anything which threatens the family. But religion sees no role in marriage for self-development. Marriage is for producing babies. Personal fulfilment in Christianity is found by holy hermits who are celibate.

'When you live together, no one takes over. It's all your own work. But marriage is a bit like cloud cuckoo land. Lots of marriages go wrong because people expect them to go right. But that's not enough. We live in a critical age. There are too many people and not enough wise people. Our system is breaking down. Therefore more people are living together to become wise. Living together helps you think about the best way to live. Marriage tells you the best way to live without argument. Living together is a way of exploring life. Couples in such arrangements don't usually have kids straight away. Married people usually have kids at once, before they know what they're doing. Living together couples usually learn enough from their experiences not to need to go out and get married.

'I object to marriage because it is unequal. If in marriage the strong protect the weak, that implies domination. I don't object to fidelity. I myself have the feeling that for depth in a relationship there is a need for a period of monogamy. But I also think that for depth in a relationship a person needs to *have had* wide sexual experience with several partners.

'I am married but separated from my first partner. I did ask Chloë when Flossie was on the way if she wanted to be my second wife but she wouldn't have me. I didn't offer very hard but she turned me down. She thinks marriage is demeaning to women. I asked in case she had reservations about bearing the child and entering the socially unfamiliar state of unwed motherhood.

'We have made mutual wills and there is a small policy in her favour and our families are delighted and supportive. So I think that side is taken care of. They take the line that we're old enough to know what we're doing. As for jealousy, I think choosing the path of cohabitation rather than marriage gives us the wisdom to deal with another relationship if it comes along. The trouble with marriage is that you expect to put the boot in. You are given a theory to apply rather than experience. The difference is between Chloë or Michael going out with someone *for a good reason*; and "my husband" or "my wife" committing "adultery". Do you see that difference?'

Ted and Mavis: making marriage equal – he *takes* her *name*

Ted lives in Lancashire. He is 55, the father of nine children from a 28-year-old marriage which ended in divorce. Four years ago he met Mavis, the love of his life and two and a half years ago no prouder man than Ted breathed in England the day he led Mavis to the altar. Not only did Ted vow to put everything right this time round, he also took Mavis' surname as a mark of his respect and desire to offer a real partnership.

'Mavis's previous husband had died but my first marriage ended while both parties were very much alive. In fact, I knew after six weeks of marrying that we should never have got together, but in those days you stuck it through. For 25 years of my life, I've been banging my head against a brick wall. My first wife had a lack of communication. She was a 23-year-old virgin when we met and

I'd been round the world. It wasn't on but fool that I was we got hitched. There was never any give and take. She couldn't be wrong. When the kids were eight or 10 they could see she was the real child – "Oh mother, grow up – things are not like that these days", they'd say.

'But Mavis is everything my first wife wasn't and to show my complete dedication to her I have taken her name and made her a financial equal in my life.

'Mavis never felt quite secure "living over the brush" (if you're posh you say "living over the hoover") so we thought we'd get properly married though we did live together for 18 months first. I say to my children "Get married when you feel you need to" and "Don't marry a person just because you want to live with them, marry them if you couldn't possibly live without them!"

'I think marriage has been too much 60/40 in the past and not enough 50/50. That tendency is in marriage itself, the way society sets it up. But Mavis is not my plaything and I am not her boss. We've tried to make marriage fit us and so far it's grand.

'We have a closed marriage, strictly faithful to each other. We don't need other couples to swap or swing. But that's because we know what our needs are because we can talk. I can honestly say to you that we know each other far better after four years than either of us knew our previous partners after two decades.

'I think most certainly marriage should be made more difficult. I say it's the only trade where you get your certificate first and the training afterwards. I tell my kids they must learn their trade as a lover. First.

'Sex is very, very important. We have sex three to four times a week (in our mid-50s), say about 10 hours devoted to love every seven days. But when you set that against the time we spend sleeping, or cooking or working, or watching telly – it's nothing. It's small in time. But it's absolutely vital to the emotional side of a relationship. Sex is not a reason for getting married. But don't get married without having had sex.

'Jealousy caused the bust-up of my marriage. I was given a bad name before I'd earned it, if you know what I mean. Jealousy is the number one cause of divorce in my book, far more important than the arrival of the children. My wife was even jealous of my children's affection for me. Jealousy is a cancer of the mind.

'I think there should be far more trial marriages before real marriage. The ceremony, the ring and the piece of paper are still important for many women. They're a part of our national folk lore. But then I think there should *also* be a private agreement about how the marriage is to work.

'For instance, I had one of my kids come to me and say "Dad, I'm pregnant, we're going to get wed now". I congratulated them (what else can you do?) on being about to produce my first grandchild but said "Look, don't get married just because you're pregnant. Get married if you really want to". They did. But one of Mavis's daughters got pregnant and didn't marry the father. She had the baby and then married someone else and now they're doing very well. I think we've gradually got to realise that people's feelings come before conventions. If they don't, the conventions will suffer more . . .'

Tina and Dennis – 'Upstairs/downstairs'

When two people with children get divorced, they should realise they are only separating. They will always be linked by their kids. They must go on seeing those kids, and must therefore talk to and meet and co-operate with each other. This, says Tina, is unavoidable. She has found what she thinks is an ideal solution to the divorce problem – at least for her children. And she hasn't even bothered to get divorced.

She is a supporter of the idea of relationships between older women and younger men, and older men and younger women, as you will see. She thinks this is more sensible than two in-experienced people getting married at 20 and making the old mistakes all over again. Besides, she says, it's incredibly sexy.

'I lived with my husband Graham for 12 months before we got married in 1960. Even then, we only got married because some friends of ours bought us a Special Licence for a birthday present. I actually forgot which day I told my mother I was going to the Registry Office and she told our relations in Australia and I suddenly received hundreds of telegrams congratulating me on my new husband when in fact we hadn't done anything about it at all. It was a hoot, but after that we *had* to go through with it.

'I'm an actress so my life tends towards chaos anyway but despite the reputation of actresses's marriages, mine was fine up to the time the children came along in the late 60s. I think if a marriage can survive kids it can survive anything. Mine couldn't.

'I stayed at home not working and looking after children for five years and I suppose Graham got used to a traditional life-style. It was too much of a shock for him when I went back to my career, and we had rows. We both got pushed into extreme positions – I called him a Buddhist freak (just cause he liked Eastern music) and he accused me of ego-tripping sex-change (because I wanted a job). We began to live entirely separate lives.

'I earned money and hung about with him "for the sake of the children". We both had affairs but didn't talk about them. We were eating separately and sleeping separately. The only thing we did together was be parents. Even then, he expected me to babysit as of right because I was the woman whereas I had to ask him, *as a special favour*, to stay in and look after the boys!

'I thought the only solution was to find another place to live where we could both have separate flats. I was lucky enough to discover this house which has three flats on different floors. I knew the only way to get him out of the old house was a compromise arrangement whereby he could still be near his children, then he'd let me use the money to get my own place.

'I think he thought he was on to a good thing. He could have sex at his girlfriend's place. Take his men friends downstairs for parties. And visit me and the family up here when the spirit moved him. It really put his nose out of joint when I started living with another man. Especially when he discovered my bloke was a 22-year-old student and I was knocking 39!

'But we've been together for two years now and it's lovely, it's wonderful. It began as overwhelming lust and that remains a big part of our affair. We take it in turns to get up and get the children off to school. Then we usually go back to bed together and make love. "God you're like a teenager again, you're like being 20" all my friends say and it's true. I was stifled in my marriage. Now it's the more you have the more you want, as they say. As I regained my security I felt more desirable.

'I love Dennis because he's beautiful but also because he loves my children. I was worried at first. They'd never seen me in bed with another man apart from their father. I used to have my men in hotels or at their place or get them out of here before breakfast. But when Dennis stayed over for the first time the boys were fine. "Ooh Daddy'll be cross when he finds out", said my eldest. "It isn't any of Daddy's business", I said. "No, Mum's right", said the other. "She's got to have her enjoyment too". So much for the wisdom of the under-10s!

'Now the children have such a good relationship with Dennis they're liable to ask him where their socks are rather than me. He has looked after them for up to five weeks at a stretch when I've been on tour and there's no other person in the world including their father I could trust to do that.

'Sometimes we have jokes about the housekeeping when I earn more than him (he's a painter). He'll say "How do you expect me to manage on what you give me?" and I say "You'll just have to make it do, dear".

'His age bothered me at first. I really like going to bed with younger men, and I thought he was about 25. Then I heard the kids asking him how old he was. They suggested 40 but when he got down to 22 before owning up I was a little taken aback. He'd said the day before he thought the woman in the middle flat was "getting on a bit" and she was only 38! But now it makes no difference. We have a relationship of equality. We're best friends. I even enjoy cooking again because he takes his turn as well.

'The real gain has been for the kids. They stay in touch with both their parents. Graham takes them on holiday to Spain. And, after a frosty start, Graham and Dennis have got together because I really think Graham admires the way Dennis copes with his children. They've even been known to sit down on a Saturday night together and watch "Match Of The Day" at Graham's.

'Dennis and I are committed to each other. I know it must end one day. There are things Dennis should do on his own. I'm not sure he still wants children after his experiences here. I won't be giving him them. But that's the only thing I can't offer.

'We're a bit too wrapped up in each other to have outside lovers though there's no agreement about it. We can't be bothered to go out at night. We just take the tv into the bedroom and cakes and drinks and have treats. Sometimes all night. It must be catching, all this pleasure, because the other day for the first time my mother asked me "What is an orgasm!".'

Martin: From commune to living together to?

Martin is 29. At 17, he left school and started working for the Post Office. He played around with radios at home and with a bit of self-taught knowledge got a job in computers at 22. Two years later he started his own Swindon-based recording studio.

'As a youngster I was rebellious and could never see the point of marriage. My parents are married and still live together but I didn't want to copy them.

'I started dating girls when I was 17, lost my virginity at 18 and went through a lot of nurses. I don't know why, but there seemed to be a lot of them around. I had a late circumcision at 25 because I had a tight foreskin but have otherwise always found sex enjoyable.

'I lived in a commune in Reading when I was 24 containing three couples and one single guy and me. I started an affair with

The meaning of marriage

'Marriage', said the Devil, 'is but a ceremonial toy'. Quite so, but it is a toy with which nearly everyone wishes to play. As we have seen, most people who can be married are married. The difficult question to decide is exactly what they've gone and done.

In the widest sense, marriage is society's recognition of the adult union of one or more males with one or more females for various purposes, for various periods of time, under various financial arrangements.

Marriages in Britain (of one man to one woman till death or divorce do them part) are no longer exclusively religious, exclusively to do with producing children nor exclusively crucial in deciding with whom we have sex or what sex roles we adopt. Not all wives work at home. Not all husbands are breadwinners. A lot of sex takes place outside marriage. Homosexuals cannot marry each other, but some priests will 'bless their relationship'. People who *cohabit* aren't married, but increasingly the laws relating to marriage (such as custody of children, access and maintenance) are applied to them regardless. So the position is complex.

Are we *monogamous*? Well, that word really means being married to one person *at a time*, despite common usage. Wolves mate for life, but humans are generally more fickle. *Monogyny* means marrying only one wife in life but there isn't a counterpart term relating to husbands. *Polygyny* was practiced by all the patriarchs of the Old Testament from Abraham to David and means having 'many wives at a time'. This, together with the much less common *polyandry* (women having many husbands at a time), are the two terms that form the concept *polygamy* (plural marriage).

In a study of 238 pre-modern societies, the anthropologist George Murdock discovered that 195 practised polygamy and only 43 mono-

one of the girls when her bloke left (it was full of university students and the turnover was quite high). Then a very special woman moved in and I took up with her and gradually the rest of the commune left. Now we live in this large ex-commune in the middle of town with more rooms than we know what to do with.

'I've always been looking for a relationship. I don't like being alone. I was on the rebound from one of my nurses when I began living with my special woman and although we love each other in a funny kind of way it's never been just plain sailing. But we are very good friends and we always will be. My son was born in 1976

gamy. Our modern system of frequent marriage and divorce is often described as *serial polygamy*. Stalwart monogynists may object to this description but with one divorce for every 3.3 new UK weddings, it is indisputably the truth.

As the institution of marriage evolved it became a means of asserting the social power of men over women. Above all, it was a way for a man to guarantee that his children were his own (by compelling his wife's fidelity) and that his own name remained immortal in the clan's memory. Marriage brought a man additional wealth in the form of a marriage gift and provided a system of transmitting that wealth to 'legitimate' heirs within the family. This system is generally described as 'patriarchy' – rule by the father.

Today, patriarchal marriage is under attack in most countries, East and West. The invention of reliable contraception (giving men *and* women sexual freedom) and the rise of women's liberation have been the main agents of change. As a result, a woman can today get married in London in a perfectly legal fashion and yet write most of the form of the marriage service and contractual vows for herself. It happens at the Unitarian Chapel in Golder's Green.

Some lawyers have also suggested the creation of a two-tier marriage system. Under this, you would be free to marry and divorce on demand. But if you decide to have children, the lawyers want you to sign a second contract with no escape clauses. They think you should be obliged to stick with your partner for the 16 years it takes a child to reach the age of marriage.

Divorce, they say, is a luxury most people in Britain cannot afford. As one solicitor remarked: 'It costs the Government £1 billion annually to service the divorce system; it would be cheaper to pay us all a bonus to stay together'.

after one miscarriage. He was well planned and we both wanted him since we're both into children.

'There was some talk of marriage at the beginning – more from me than her – but there didn't seem to be much reason. It would have been more to satisfy our parents than anything else. We have no rules drawn up as such; I've made some financial arrangements for the boy.

'I'd like the relationship to work out. My job isn't stable, steady and predictable. This causes some tension. But whatever tough times we've been through have had nothing to do with us turning our backs on marriage. Things would have been no better and might well have been worse if we'd been married. Not being married means we can have "flexible" disputes. Nobody has to say "This isn't the way you treat a wife, or a husband".

'If ever I became a millionaire I might get married for a gas, as an idea for a party, I suppose. But the serious answer is I doubt if we will. If my son got persecuted at school because he was illegitimate, I'd think again.

'The problem with marriage is that people think it's going to do something for you. If I'm not married, I remain an individual. The absurdity of the marriage ceremony gets me down – so full of wild promises. By not marrying, I am saying to the world that my morals are up to me to decide – not you. I don't respect non-believers who go running to the church as soon as they fancy a wedding – or a funeral.

'What does piss me off though is the fact that I can't claim for a wife on my income tax. But then is THAT the reason for getting married – so you can claim on your income tax?'

G.N. Single misery

'On the face of it I have everything going for me: a comfortable middle class background, public school and I have just graduated from university with a first class degree. However, my personal life is an absolute disaster in that I have never managed to develop any kind of relationship with persons of either gender.

'It is so depressing to go into the pub and see those all around me chatting away with friends and entering into conversations with complete strangers. All I can manage is to quaff my pint and stare at some "interesting" architectural feature. I just cannot bring myself to enter into conversation always fearing a rebuff and I consciously consider myself to be inferior to all and sundry.

'When it comes to females despite the fact that I am nearly 23 I have never spoken to one in a social context. I am always gripped by a terrible feeling of inadequacy, always believing that the female would be angered by any approach by me.

'The most frustrating aspect of my own character is the habit of frosting people out or even being lost for words. This only occurs in social contexts and people who are acquainted with me at work just would not accept the reality of my own isolation.

'Misery is compounded by the fact that everyday life is crammed with totems of my own failure: couples walking hand in hand down the street. One cannot imagine the effect of seeing happy couples; it only serves to emphasise my despair.

'God knows what is to be done to break the situation into which I have fallen, but it is having a deleterious effect upon my life. I am drinking heavily – in my flat – and I am beginning to question my very raison d'etre.'

Thus the cycle is re-born. For all our efforts to promote intimacy and new relationships, our world is at this moment making new men with defective systems of communication who cannot address the opposite sex as fellow-creatures. So long as failure is unmanly, this youth must remain mute or risk his masculinity. Yet as we shall see in the next chapter concerning sex, the cure is worse than the cold. Defining silence as strength deprives men of life's principal skills – the ability to understand, explain, reflect, learn and change.

5 The Overburdened Penis

'When Nerina Shute's mother was married she spent her first night in the Charing Cross Hotel, London, on her way to France. Her husband, a kindly enough fellow, appeared before her in the bedroom, told her she looked pretty, and shortly afterwards said: "You know what has to be done, so don't make a fuss".' Duncan Crow, *The Edwardian Woman*, 1978)

'She is slow to rouse, once or twice a year, possibly four times, I find heaven in *her* unspeakable sweet joy. *Can it be oftener? Can it be fairly regular?* I am afraid too often I bore her and that ends by boring me inexpressibly. Single lust is a feeble squib. I want fireworks!' (An Essex vicar to Dr Marie Stopes, May 1919)

'It is very vulnerable even when made of stone, and the museums of the world are filled with herculean figures brandishing penises that are chipped, clipped or completely chopped off' (Gay Talese, *Thy Neighbour's Wife*, 1980)

'Frank Chapple might say in one breath that Neil Kinnock *has* balls and, in the next, that Roy Hattersley or Eric Heffer or Peter Shore *talks* balls. To possess balls is to succeed; to express balls (especially in loads) is to fail miserably' (Anna Coote, *New Statesman*, 16/9/1983)

'A man is supposed to be ever-ready, like the battery' (quoted by Uta West, *If Love Is The Answer, What Is The Question?*, 1977)

'Masturbation: sex with someone you love' (Woody Allen)

If men confuse masculinity with power, think what they do with sexuality. Here is the greatest irony in erotic history. If men can't have sex, they think they lack puissance. The very label they have chosen for this state – 'impotence' meaning 'lack of power' – indicates how their minds work. And yet most of the mechanisms of male sexuality are not amenable to conscious acts of will. Even if you reduce sex to a matter of male conquest, you cannot force the pace. A high proportion of rapists, for instance, experience functional impotence. At the basest level, therefore, it behoves men on their own assumptions of masculine dominance to learn how to become more sexual. And the argument applies all the way up the scale.

The best way to convey this to bewildered males is to ask, 'What is an erection?'. Answer: predominantly a reflex. A man cannot *choose* to have an erection. He can only choose those circumstances which are favourable to the having of erections. This is because the oldest part of the brain is generally in charge of sexual response, not the modern 'freer-thinking' cerebral cortex. Sex is more of a subliminal drive than a rational thought. That is why men day-dream about sex at least once an hour and dream about it during sleep at least twice as often as anything else. In purely biological terms, therefore, a virile man must possess a modicum of passivity, often regarded as a feminine trait. He must wait for a sexy stimulus to strike home in the right place at the right time and then – provided there is no other fear, threat, danger or preoccupation – his erection will take care of itself. After all, an erection is only the pumping of more blood into the hollow spaces of the penis than is allowed to flow out again. It is a routine procedure under normal circumstances, but still amazingly difficult for some men to understand. Perhaps a male military metaphor will help.

Whenever General Brain at HQ perceives an attractive target person to be within range, he is obliged by the constitution to issue a complex list of standing orders. Among these are electro-chemical instructions to the valves regulating penile blood-flow. Rapidly, the army's advance guard comes to attention. Phallic formation is achieved. The nation's manhood strains to effect a capture. However, standing orders also include a strict proviso to 'stand down' should any enemy opposition be encountered. Even if a single tank (equivalent perhaps to a noise in the street) appears on General Brain's mental horizon, the whole process may be shifted into reverse. Erection retreats. Blood flows from the penis to the large muscles of the body. After all, blood is the universal foot soldier and may be required to pump the muscles to action if the sensitive male is physically threatened by the cause of that street-noise (a returning husband?). The same is true if General Brain is ordered to carry out any Higher Priority Work.

Such work all too often includes a request by the brain's owner to think about the act of sex – 'Will I make it this time? Will I fail like last time? Does she/he really fancy me? Am I doing it properly? Have I got BO? Has she/he been unfaithful to me?'. All these highly conscious considerations override and countermand the processes of male sexual arousal. All human brains are trained to treat survival as being of higher priority than sexual pleasuring. There may even be evidence to show that male brains are trained to give higher priority to *any* task of problem-solving over sexual pleasuring. Be that as it may, the primary cause of impotence is the loss of inner confidence by men at those times when doubts abound.

In summary, General Brain quite correctly sees sex as a rewarding but un-intellectual peace-time activity. It is consequently a great help if the rewards can be stressed and drawbacks minimised by a partner's stroke of the highly sensitive skin of the penis (and elsewhere) so that waves of pleasure are sent back through the body telling the brain to cool down and join the party. This is because sustained erection requires both psychological *and* physical input, both fantasy *and* friction, and this in turn is because the human sexual response is hooked into the involuntary, autonomic nervous system. Life would indeed be simpler for men if getting an erection were a *muscular* action controlled by the will, like pointing a finger. But it's not, it's a hydraulic system triggered off by a reflex. This helps keep us human and prevents cramp in a crisis.

Therefore, no man can put his hand on what Sigmund Freud called the 'executive organs of sexuality' and honestly claim they have never let him down. I can't. Second World War US commander General Eisenhower couldn't according to his aide and driver, Kate Summersby. Novelist Simon Raven can't ('Years of brandy and baccarat have left me semi-impotent'). Even James Bond can't – 'For an hour in that room with Le Chiffre the certainty of impotence had been beaten into him and a scar had been left that could only be healed by experience' (Ian Fleming, *Casino Royale*, 1953). Solly, a 70-year-old taxi-driver, can't – 'Staring mournfully at his prick and intoning "We were born together. We grew up together. We got married together. Why, oh why did you have to die before me?"' (*Spectator*). Daniel Khanu of Nairobi certainly can't – 'His wife stabbed him to death on 14th October because he was impotent' (*East African Standard*). J. Reginald Christie, mass-killer, once of *10 Rillington Place* (Ludovic Kennedy, 1961), couldn't ('"Reggie-No-Dick", as he was called, could only copulate with the still-warm bodies of his female victims'). Two and a half thousand readers of the *Daily Star* on 1st December, 1980, who sent for my leaflet on impotence can't and, according to some estimates, several million Americans and many thousands of Britons can't. That adds up to a massive leaning tower of personal grief topped with some irony when readers write to people like me about their 'long-standing problem'. I could weep twice over, because male potency is not, of course, essential to good sex. Love-making should embrace the whole body using the whole body's largest organ, the skin, and its biggest sex organ, the imagination. So what if the penis is non-tumescent? You have hands and mouth to procure orgasms galore and a sense of touch to make your pulses reel.

Nevertheless, most heterosexual couples wish to find themselves in the throes of regular sexual intercourse, and I have nothing but sympathy for those who are unable to. If a couple want to start a family, I feel strongly for the man whose inability to complete the sex act reduces the chances of fertilisation. It is only when a man complains of impotence as a result of using his penis as a 'weapon' of dominance over the woman, that I find it difficult to identify, especially where the sex resembles rape. Over the years, I have received several hundred letters from men asking why they cannot perform with women they seem to fear, want to master or affect to despise. I remember the particular grouse of one young man who was appalled with his penis for 'failing with a bird' he 'didn't fancy a bit' although he'd decided to 'give it a go' in order to keep his 'sex-life up to scratch'. The way he described things, his sex-life sounded like a series of outward bound activities leading to a final examination in technique.

He could, of course, blame it on the historic masculine bias of sex researchers, at least one of whom defines impotence as the:

> 'persistent inability to develop and/or maintain a penile erection sufficient to conclude intercourse to the satisfaction of the male'.

No mention of feelings there (and the implied definition of

'satisfactory' intercourse *could* encompass rape). Obviously, being impotent is quite different from being 'premature', but many women would argue from their end of the bed that it amounts to the same thing. One of Marie Stopes' correspondents saw the problem like this 60 years ago:

> 'You emphasise . . . the importance of conjugal intercourse being a joint act, i.e. the gratification of the discharge should not be confined to the male, but should be shared by the female . . . But the difficulty must often be that the discharges do not coincide in time. If that of the woman is late, it is difficult to see what ought to be done, as to prolong coition would be for the man a serious strain . . .'
> (Rev. E. Lyttleton to Marie Stopes, August 1920).

If a woman in a good relationship needs one hour of intercourse to reach climax, is the man 'impotent' if he can sustain himself for no more than half an hour and cannot get a second erection? The woman might say yes. The man might disagree.

He could add that impotence is especially bewildering for both sexes since 'failure', as I have implied, is *normal* for all men sometimes. This is the most difficult lesson to get across to an angry, frustrated woman and to those Burt Reynolds' clones who seem to regard their bodies as two-speed power drills with hammer actions. Certainly, it helps to know what Manly Man does not – that the sexual current is switched off late at night, after too much booze, with the wrong partner, when the telephone rings or as the mind wanders. A man can lose his erection in certain sex positions if the stimulation is insufficient to excite him, if his partner does not make it clear she is enjoying his attentions or, as I suggest, if her husband comes home and taps him menacingly on the left buttock.

In fact, fully two thirds of male impotence is due to this psychological anxiety of performance pressure. Paradoxically, this is a state of disgrace as far as the manly stereotype is concerned; yet the male sex can only blame itself:

> 'Of the men we see, most . . . are so focused on . . . being "real" men that they make love when they don't want to . . . when they are too tense and uncomfortable to be able to respond . . .' (Bernie Zilbergeld, *Men and Sex*, 1978).

A man may terrorise himself into impotence because he would rather admit, if he must, to being a non-starter than a novice.

Others are schizoid, separating head from private parts or making love largely to admire their own magnificence. It's a surprise when they discover that emotionless sex very soon becomes motionless sex. The killer Christie was obviously more extreme. His perverted personality, damaged from birth, literally divorced sex from life. But the common element is that all such men feel anxiety in place of desire.

The same disorder of response is true in cases of premature or inhibited ejaculation. In fact, almost all male sexual problems are primed by panic whereas most of women's difficulties can be attributed to simple taboo. The mighty male has nearly always been encouraged to sow his wild oats and the lowly female to hoard hers. And yet he is the one with the greater neuroticism. When ejaculation misfires, it is because nervousness has blended with sexual arousal. The man is either half-way to orgasm before any clothes have been removed since fear has pre-stimulated him, or panic has so overloaded the nervous pathways that the sexual command to 'fire' is not obeyed because it cannot be heard.

Tension from whatever source is equivalent to background arousal of the sexual system, and yet we have already seen that stress tends to diminish sexual capacity. A man may well find that his state of mind simply inhibits erection. What he may also be surprised to discover is that while stress reduces this aspect of sexuality, it increases the likelihood of ejaculation. Irony rules. It is perfectly possible for such a man to have *either* a sort of spontaneous emission without erection, *or* an instant climax upon erection *without prior warning*.

Orgasmic mishaps of this sort are usually associated with a lifestyle where sex is subordinated to utility ('I *need* sexual outlets . . . men *need* more sex than women . . . I *need* to make female conquests') though the price paid is a fundamental breakdown of communication between the brain and the genitals to parallel the loss of sexual control. A man's standard defence in these circumstances is to take refuge in the manly stereotype, most eloquently summarised in my view by the cartoon showing a rather pompous-looking businessman in bed with a disgruntled-looking young woman: 'Of course I ejaculate prematurely', he says, 'I'm a very busy man'.

Such bluster is unable to offer lasting solace mainly because your partner remains disgruntled, in which case there is no alternative but to revise masculine ideals of bedroom behaviour. If men would eschew the grand performance, if they would cease to compare themselves with predecessors who cannot logically be their 'rivals', then they should at last be able to dissipate sufficient inner tension to hear what their bodies are saying to them. They can listen. This eventually clears the background static and finally they may fire at will.

This listening craft is crucial. I recall one client arriving with his wife for help with the problem of premature ejaculation who found it imperative to hold the floor on all occasions. Even when we asked *her* a question, *he* would reply. It was almost impossible for him – as a man – to stop taking responsibility for everything going on around him or connected with his marriage and family, practically insulting his wife's intelligence in the process. When we suggested he start experimenting with silences, he heard that his partner was displeased with more than their sex life. We began to work on these conflicts. He began to discover that his wife had requirements in the bedroom of her own. He began to hear from her that it takes two to make love in an equal partnership. He learned from us how to stop being a very busy man in bed. Gradually, he began to get in touch with his own sexual feelings, instead of hearing an order to 'be the dutiful conjugal leader'.

Having grasped that it is not an essential part of the male role to run the sexual show, this man also learned that he was not – in an ultimate sense – bound to take responsibility for his wife's orgasm; he had to look after his own. By worrying about whether she was going to come, he made damn sure he did too soon and that she couldn't. Sex, he began to see, is not something men do to women but something men and women mutually generate. Eventually, we got this frenetic managing director to return home earlier in the evening in order to give more time to the childcare (which he enjoyed), and even to stop gobbling his food as though time's winged chariots were about to run him over. He says he is a happier man today (who can last as long as he likes during sex); he has resigned as conjugal leader and no longer threatens his penis with death if it falls asleep on duty.

Yet in overt and subtle ways, a great many men still hang their entire identity from this appendage, thereby warning the penis never to fail or else. Such genital terrorism precludes focus on the remainder of the body, enough to ignore the tremendous erotic potential of hands and feet, for instance, which are connected to areas of brain almost as large as those servicing the genitals. Moreover, tactile contact across the body is essential to good health. Untouched babies may even suffer brain damage.

Untouched men begin to suffer damaged sensibilities. Men who are only touched on the penis, and rarely 'permit' touch elsewhere because it feels too threatening, are bound to overburden a sexual system prone to inhibition at the first signs of anxiety.

They are also bound to make more of the organ in question than common sense sanctions. For a long time, Western Europe ordained fig leaves for its statuary because, as one woman quipped, the penis was 'too important to be cheapened by public exposure' (Phyllis Chesler, *About Men*, 1978). Men also refuse to dwell too long on the fact that the penis is, in one sense, merely an elongated clitoris with an additional urethral function and that the scrotum is only formed from the fusing of what would otherwise have turned out to be a perfectly healthy pair of vaginal lips. There, but for the intercession of pre-natal hormones, goes every lord and master.

Men who equate themselves with their *penes*, also trap themselves into a rebellion against nature. As they wish to enhance their status, so they say they want bigger genitals, almost wishing the private parts were responsive to fertiliser. Hence the riches of charlatans with pills, potions and penis-developers of various kinds promising to augment length and girth by return of post. It is not unknown (*General Practitioner*, 31/7/1981) for a man to inject paraffin into his penis to enlarge the shaft and increase the duration of erection. Polystyrene rods may be inserted by a plastic surgeon for the same purpose. Other men depend on the efficacy of galvanic electricity or even hang weights on the end. Elastic bands also play their bizarre part. . .

What is so sad about all this, apart from the commercial racketeering and the impossibility of success, is the assumption common to men who think they are too 'small' that they are thereby condemned to insignificance as human beings:

'Having heard you on the radio I have decided to ask your advice after many years of frustration and misery.

I was an extremely shy person as a child and until I was in my middle 20s, because of this shyness, I did not let other people look at me in the WC and neither did I have the courage to look at them and so I was not aware of how small my penis was. At 24 I got married and I had conquered a little of my shyness and until that time I had not had sex at all nor did I masturbate.

After a period of marriage and conversation with my wife and others I realised what a miserable sexual specimen I was and was happy to have been married and enjoyed some sex although my wife admitted later in our lives that she had had an affair with another man early on in our marriage.

I have been a widower for five years and have often wished to get acquainted with a woman with prospects of sex and perhaps to settle down again in marriage. But now that I am aware of my inadequacy, there is no way that I can start taking a woman out. My children cannot understand why I want nothing to do with women and I can assure you it is not because I don't like them. Friends have tried to get me paired off, but of course I decline.

I would undergo surgery if anything can be done to alter my miserable state . . . I am now 53 and missed a lot from life . . .'

Now the facts in this sad but not untypical problem history are that the man's sexual organs, upon medical examination, were of perfectly normal dimensions but a chronic sense of personal inadequacy had become fixated solely on his genital size. His shyness, his wife's affair, his widowerhood, lack of female companionship and the suggested surgical solution – all these are phallus-related. Perhaps his wife made some disparaging remark about his penis as a way of rationalising her own guilt about having had an extra-marital affair, or as a shorthand for complaining about his poor sexual technique, but certainly the idea struck her husband with the force of a bomb that here was the obvious explanation of all that had ever gone wrong. For him it stood to reason – because men in our culture are phallo-centric. Men say women suffer from penis envy but it is *they* who are the ones impressed by other men's monstrosities. It is not enough that men possess the largest sexual organs of all the male primates. Those who support the sexual stereotype despite the damage it may do them insist on still more. One wonders whether they'd be satisfied with Beardsleyesque phalluses of such dimensions they need to be carried in both hands.

This cult of what we might call the 'Neurotic Penis', where men only derive their identity from their genitality, extends into a further subculture of male sexual anxieties. Put briefly, if this *is* your identity, you automatically fixate on it. I get letters from men perturbed about circumcision, lack of circumcision, curvature of the penis where no illness is implicated (as it is in the very rare Peyronie's syndrome), about the uneven hang of the testicles (which is normal), about the oily sebaceous glands in the penile skin, about the vigour of ejaculation and the quantity of the ejaculate. Suffice it to say that, whatever the force of the argument for phallo-dominance, the manly stereotype in this respect particularly is responsible for more misery than pleasure. If you want a personal reference, I myself have never been able to decide whether or not the penis and testicles are intrinsically ridiculous to behold when contrasted with the neat anatomy of women. It is certainly difficult to run with an erection and painful to run naked whether the penis is flaccid or engorged. And if you want an ultimate perspective on the idea of female penis envy, share my admiration for the little girl who, upon seeing her first penis, remarked:

'Mother, isn't it a blessing they don't have them on their faces?'

There is one advantage to having a set of external genitals which should never be belittled. For males, sex comes to hand. They learn the virtues of manual exploration from an early age. In the process, they also learn its vices, some of which I have been indirectly discussing, such as phallic reductionism. And yet it is men who quickly establish familiarity with their personal pattern of arousal and response, albeit speedy and rough, whereas women sometimes fail to acquire this important knowledge. Men have got it right when it comes to assessing sex as natural behaviour which sensible people can enjoy. Where they may go too far is in detaching sex from reciprocity and in pretending to know all about human sexuality when they are merely skin-deep experts on their own. It is a fatal but common mistake, for example, for men to assume that a woman's sexuality must be the same as a man's simply because the notion of sexual omni-competence is built into the male identity. Many men feel compelled to advance the insupportable thesis that virility and sexual incompetence are incompatible. In fact, the news is that virile men are often quite clueless in bed.

If the equation of male sexuality with power causes individual difficulties, it is impossible to ignore the profound social consequences. Surveying the male-focused sex industry, we have to ask whether the masculine power-drive corrupts the world at large? At the very least, men appear to sacrifice quality to quantity. One of the fabled differences between the sexes is that:

'While women want a lot of sex from the man they love, men want a lot of sex from a lot of different women' (Anon.).

From the depths of male didacticism, the poet Coleridge offers this related thought:

'The man's desire is for the woman; but the woman's desire is rarely other than for the desire of the man' (*Biographia Literaria*, 23/7/1827).

If it is true that the woman wishes to engage the affections of the man, while the man only wishes to possess the woman, then the sexes are set in a pattern of damaging social conflict.

Of course, this divergence yields much of the spice of life, and nobody wants identical sexes, but if men only seek possession, there is no compelling reason why they should ever call it a day. Possess one, you might say, possess them all. *Possess* one and women have successfully been defined as property:

'If you long for your wife to be laid by another man I would be happy to oblige. Aged 43, unpossessive, discreet . . .' (*Forum*, July 1983).

Promiscuity is not inherently corrupt for there are men and women with very high sexual drives, impeccable manners, a horror of commercial entanglements, a penchant for sensuality, a disinclination for matrimony, a scrupulous regard for questions of consent, a diligence in matters of hygiene and a gift for intimate friendship. Yet it has to be said that such paragons are few and far between. More common are Casanovas with chips on their shoulders. Men overall are still more promiscuous than women. Kinsey (*Sexual Behaviour in the Human Male*, 1948), for instance, reported that on average the American male at marriage had enjoyed 1523 orgasms to the average American female's 223 – a gap that is closing) and much of male promiscuity is founded on imperial greed – the lust for conquest. As a result, men frequently abuse sex as a means of achieving dominance over women who frequently regard sex as a means of registering a friendship. This reinforces an important measure of confusion in human affairs. It causes a lot of pain to some women. And it traps innumerable men on a treadmill of tedious polygamy. However hard you try, you cannot fuck everyone and your vaunted domination is doomed to remain incomplete. By denying their need for reciprocal intimacy (which does not preclude masturbation, love affairs or serial marriage) men lose more than they gain, turn sex into work and flirt with the 'new impotence' of satiety.

If you want classic modern examples, look no further than the attitudes of US President Lyndon B. Johnson:

> '. . . coming back into the room naked after a shower [he] would take his penis in his hand, and say: "Well, I've gotta take 'ole Jumbo here and give him some exercise. I wonder who I'll fuck tonight' (Robert A. Caro, *The Years Of Lyndon Johnson*, 1982).

Or ponder the case – for it is one – of French crime writer Georges Simenon, creator of 'Inspector Maigret' and author of 214 books, who announced in an interview in 1977 that he had made love to more than 10,000 women in his adult lifetime, which amounted to more than three females weekly, for 52 weeks a year, over a period of 61 years. Even a slow-witted detective could see at once that a man who was *also* producing three and a half books a year in the same period was either skimping on his work, which on the evidence seems unlikely, or somehow failing to investigate the in-depth personal reality of his paramours. The author's alibi for his gluttony would convince neither judge nor jury. He suggested he had 'loved women' all his life and claimed to be perennially interested in 'human communication'. The prosecution is quick to reply that 'love' like that merely gives abbreviation a bad name and if he wanted to communicate so much why leave so little time to talk.

The truth later emerged in a study by Fenton Bresler (*The Mystery of Georges Simenon*, 1979) that Simenon was compensating for feelings of inferiority with women through his own private philosophy of phallic dominance. He preyed on secretaries and serving girls and paid in cash for the majority of his encounters. The key to his compulsion was fear. He felt he couldn't be sure a woman was not laughing at him until he had changed her expression from one of imagined hauteur to orgasmic craving. He was curious, but it was an encapsulated curiosity about himself. Naturally enough, there was no answer to his enquiries since the horizontal experiments never developed into learning experiences. If you always remain in control, you do not gain effective feedback from others about your behaviour. It readily calls to mind the typical male harem fantasy, with our hero surrounded by a modest 37 sex slaves, to the first of whom he turns and says: 'I love you, pass it on . . .'. No danger of reciprocity there either.

When this fantasy impinges on harder social reality, we find men are the ones who give unequivocal evidence of wishing to divorce sex from feelings in general, as though their primal terror was of personal involvement. In every major prostitution centre, it is men who copulate with anonymous women on street corners or in cars. Throughout the free world, it is men who purchase pornographic filmstock featuring nameless fantasy females or even just their unattributed private parts. It is scientifically true that women can be aroused by pornography. They are known to patronise male striptease shows. They buy large quantities of vibrators. And they masturbate. But no one has yet been able to make a wholesale business out of selling prostitution and pornography to women. *Playgirl* publishes photos of superstuds but retains a large market amongst America's male homosexuals. *Cosmopolitan* sells the psychology of sexual *relationships* to its liberated readers but had to discontinue an early flirtation with the nude male gatefold (commencing with Mr Germaine Greer, funnily enough) and women's pulp fiction in paperback finds it necessary to exploit romance, not sex, for its hard cash. In men's publishing, by contrast, the market prefers action, performance and adventure to insight, and women are treated as toys.

It is not the existence of pornography and prostitution themselves, but the social denial of women's humanity in the way we organise them that measures men's corruption. It would be perfectly possible, as in classical days, to produce an egalitarian religious or humanistic system of prostitution for all. In a similar spirit, modern Western countries might sanction the production of unobjectionable artificial aids to erotic arousal. It would only be necessary to remain aware that we are all sexual subjects to permit more of us to recall that we are also sexual objects since we can only perceive each other through our senses. But it is this sexual subjectivity or autonomy of women that appears to terrify men.

One suggestion is that the real problem is male disgust with sex itself, rather than traditional fears of castration. On this analysis, men are super-squeamish conservatives who cannot come to terms with the existence of creatures fashioned differently from themselves. They are appalled by the forces of menstruation, for example, symbolising women's childbirth prerogatives over men and their pseudo-supernatural ability to bleed and live. They are equally horrified to hear that woman's sexual capacity is now known to exceed their own. A competitive ego may well have to oppose a woman's erotic demands if he suspects that she can always beat him hollow in any fair contest of stamina. The 'refractory' period between climaxes is no 'woman's weakness'; she can always have more orgasms than a man.

Yet the true terror probably goes deeper still, straight to the core of men's emotions, beyond all the statistical generalisations. The male sex is mainly at pains to treat women like pretty androids because they – we – live in mortal terror of defencelessness. If we lose control of sex, we may involuntarily lose our hearts. We will certainly end up face to face with our feelings of vulnerability, loss, incapacity, inferiority and powerlessness. And what could we do then? What if we made a real encounter with ourselves minus the masculine shield? We would enter the madness of subordination, of being nothing, of breaking down. This is what frightens men. A manly man has to amount to something outside himself or collapse.

So, we assert rights we don't morally possess in order to maintain a position that deprives us of attachments we secretly covet. The masculine man's *lack of emotion* is often paradoxical evidence of powerful hidden desires. It takes a lot of energy to feign heroic imperturbability. When men do let go, it is of the greatest significance in my view that they tend to fall in love more quickly than women and out of love far more slowly. They have the greatest possible hunger for love and go to the greatest lengths to conceal their appetite. They suffer from the maximum sense of insecurity in the process.

Between whiles, the selfish penis thrives or believes it does. Men think about sex more than six times an hour between the ages of 35–40 twice every hour between 40 and 50 once an hour between 50 and 60 (Brothers, *What Every Woman Should Know About Men*, 1982). They look at women on the street in a visual hunt for the best body. They look at breasts, bottoms and the lips of genitals suggested through trousers. They are always looking, always checking the externals, wondering what they can do to 'it', wondering what they can get from 'it', in a game of constant sexual video. In their language, they betray a sort of self-centred schizophrenia. The women they see who might be sexually available turn into 'tarts' and 'slags', 'easy lays' and 'scrubbers'.

Those they can't have instantly become 'prick-teasers', 'ball-breakers' and 'man-eaters'. If sexual connection is achieved, the 'bird is pulled' with connotations of removing the guts from Christmas turkeys.

> 'After you've been with one like, after you've done it like, well they're scrubbers afterwards, they'll go with anyone. I think it's that once they've had it, they want it all the time, no matter who it's with . . . the lads are after the "easy lay" at dances, though they think twice about being seen to "go out" with them' (quoted by Paul Willis, *Learning To Labour*, 1978).

In bed, it is masculine to be sexual but effeminate to be affectionate. As we have seen, fearlessness is enjoined on men but fearfulness is often the result. The selfish penis is attached to a selfish lover. Since men are quick to arouse, they want women to be ready in the same lapse of time. By and large, women aren't. Preparatory cuddles are viewed by men as a boring interlude. Freud may have described foreplay as the 'kindling sticks of sex' but a lot of men seem fearful of getting their fingers burnt. The manly man insists the sex starts now, always initiates the event, always chooses the position and always decides when it's finished. More than one stand-up comic has seen to the heart of this routine. The joke is put into the mouth of a daughter asking this awkward question:

> 'Mum, what's an orgasm?'
> 'Dunno, luv, ask your father'.

I still hear stories from women about men who roll over and sleep after climaxing regardless of the state of the woman's desires, as though sex *was* male orgasm.

In their sexual fantasies, the manly men concentrate on conjuring women who yearn for rape-like intercourse, submissively soliciting the 'big one'. More than one commentator has pointed out that this tends to justify male sexual aggression, lack of commitment and hasty retreat to the male world as soon as the deed is done:

> 'The notion that women *want* to be overcome by force has been contradicted by almost every reputable sex researcher and psychiatrist yet the notion perseveres, despite the fact

that it excludes almost all the elements that most women look for in a successful sexual experience' (Michael Korda, *Male Chauvinism! Power! Success!*, 1980).

The selfish penis is often hell-bent in bed on acting out a scenario entirely lodged in its owner's brain. It is perhaps fashionable to quote Freud's:

'When two people make love, there are at least four people present – the two making love and the two they are thinking about'

but erotic solipsism is not quite what he had in mind.

The ability to function unilaterally is only an asset to the lying philanderer or prig. There are men who can make spine-tingling love, vow constancy, share their hearts, appear tender; they rise from the bed, attach their cufflinks, blow a kiss from the door and erase the matter from their minds as they set foot in the street. Such bifurcating ability borders on the psychotic. Their brothers in the imperial school of fornication 'bifurcate' on the question of the double moral standard. They argue that adultery is correct for men but wrong for women since a man *gains* territory through infidelity but can only *lose* it through the infidelity of his female partner. Women in this world, you may have gathered, are some sort of geopolitical stamping-ground.

I am happy to submit all this information because I remain convinced that life between the sexes does not always follow this pattern. Many men have avoided stereotyping. Giles Evans complained to the *Guardian*:

'I have found your articles disturbing and unsatisfactory because . . . you persist in attacking men as some sort of universal type . . . I find it offensive that you persist in lumping me in the same category as the rest of my sex. You are not treating me as a person' (12/10/1978).

Good for Giles, although one exception does not invalidate the grounds for generalisation. More cuttingly, another man recently protested to the *New Statesman* à propos its debate on masculinity that he had never been anything but illogical in his dealings with life and couldn't grow a stiff upper lip if he tried.

The fact remains that we all possess choices, even the manly men. They are free to go on insisting on their right to dominance for as long as they can get away with it, but they will have to pay the price. Men who say

'I can't function if the sexual decisions are ever in the woman's hands' (*Executive Magazine*, April 1982)

will only receive the limited pleasure of sex on sufferance with little spontaneous feedback of love and warmth. The ever-present risk is that the shop (or territory) will eventually be closed to them altogether. On the other hand, men can sing a new song of sex, transposing their anxieties. The lyrics go: 'Surprise me . . .' or 'You're here too: this is just as much for you as it is for me' or 'Tonight we'll just please you . . .'or 'You want to make love and I don't particularly, so we will but I don't want to come'. If men expose their humanity, they'll discover their sexuality:

'The real basis for a sexual relationship is to reduce things to the level of one-to-one, while at the same time slowing down the world. The key element is time, which is of course the one thing that almost nobody has to spare, except for things of lesser importance' (Korda, 1980).

Cases

Here are just a few insights from various sources into the problematic world of male sexuality.

The following extract is taken from a column I used to write for the *Daily Star*:

'Far too many men believe sex is something done *by* men *to* women. What they ignore is that love is a two-way exchange. People are miserable if they have no one to give them love and attention. But lots of others, especially women, are fed up because they have no one to *take* their love. This is just another form of selfishness. If your lover is all give and no take, show him this letter and my answer.'

'My boyfriend is 21 and I'm 20. We live together and everything is great except for one thing – sex!

'I hardly know what to do to make it exciting for him. In fact I get the feeling I'm a great big bore in bed. I know he loves me, and he says I turn him on. But how can I believe it when I don't do anything to him?

'It's always me that gets all the attention. I've never had an orgasm with him, but he keeps insisting we'll get there with a bit more effort.

'Please tell me what turns a man on.'

My reply:

'Men vary, but many get turned on simply by turning on their partners. That's why they are desperate for the woman to reach orgasm.

'But this isn't good enough if the woman ends up feeling like a laboratory experiment. Where's the fun in lying back admiring someone else's technique?

'You are in this position, and it's draining you of confidence. And you cannot climax because you no longer believe you are sexy.

'Your boyfriend behaves in this way to boost his own confidence, but you've got to stop him playing the strong silent type.

'Next time he wants to make love, give him a sensual massage instead of intercourse. What's more, he's got to let you know how it feels as you touch him.

'You'll begin to discover what turns him on. Let him know that the sooner he lets you give him pleasure, the sooner you will enjoy climaxes *together*.' (*Daily Star*, 12/10/1981).

*   *   *

Men are the fetishistic sex *par excellence*. Various theories seek to explain the cause, the most popular being the 'overspill' view. This suggests that men fixate on any object or circumstance associated with sex if (a) their sex drive is so high it cannot be satisfied through conventional channels; or (b) if normal sex is so anxiety-laden for them they'd rather avoid it. Thus shoes, handbags, stockings, rings, underwear – literally any item associated with women and sex – can become the trigger for initial male arousal. In the process of fetishising a man often views a woman as an 'un-person', as in this case:

'Postman John Hansford liked girls who wore glasses. But all he wanted to do was to snatch the spectacles off their faces. Which he did, to 38 young women over two years.

Sometimes he wore a black mask when he crept up behind girls and grabbed their glasses. Occasionally he would brandish a knife, but mostly he would simply talk to the girl on some pretext and then suddenly make a snatch for their glasses. He would nearly always smash the glasses on the spot before running away.

Psychiatrist Dr Patrick Galway told the court that this was an impulsive fetish. He reckoned it would take up to five years psychiatric treatment to cure him.

Hansford's wife, who was wearing glasses, listened to the evidence.

Mr Robert Wheatley, prosecuting said Hansford told the police: 'I don't really know why I did it. I just fancy girls who wear glasses.'

He had even walked into a house and grabbed the glasses off the speechless housewife standing there. In a statement to police he said: 'I didn't mean to do any harm. I just wanted to get their glasses off.' (*Daily Mail*, 3/3/1979, reprinted by permission of the Press Association Ltd.).

*   *   *

Male sexual fantasies wander even further afield than the cosy perspectives of the world of optometry. What is most bizarre about them is the constant reiteration of the desire to escape the role of masterful dominator. A reversal of the power balance is given an exciting erotic charge when a man who normally clings to his prerogatives surrenders them, usually to a muscular female martinet. Note, however, that this variety of fantasy could not work for non-chauvinists.

'Most of my fantasies centre on erotic domination by the opposite sex . . . usually [they] involve a situation where a rather buxomly attractive girl compels me to submit to 'punishment' in the form of spanking. These fantasies involve a lot of ritual and psychological as well as physical domination. They always lead to intercourse with the woman ending up as excited by the spanking as I am. They usually begin something like this . . .' (G.P., Birmingham).

*   *   *

In the last resort, it is men themselves who pay a very high price for their impenetrable masculinity. I could fill a separate book with tales from men of their sexual disasters. Suffice it here to say that the following 'victims' either suffer from self-inflicted guilts (often about masturbation) or self-enlarged panics (often about impotence) and sometimes they suffer from both.

'I am a 17-year-old virgin and I hope that you can help me with a problem that I have. As far as I know, I function perfectly normally but the other night I tried to have sex with my girlfriend, yet I wouldn't let her touch me because I didn't have an erection even though she was lying there naked.

This is worrying me considerably and I wonder if it is anything to do with the fact that I was very nervous at the time or that I used to masturbate quite a lot when I was younger . . .'

'I am 63 years of age and now get the sexual urge about every two months which as far as I am aware is normal. I am in good health and still manage to play a round of golf. Could you please tell me if there is anything I could take which would increase sexual desire? I see creams and pills in sex shops but I do not trust these as they may injure health . . .'

*   *   *

I find it interesting that the latter gentleman had considered taking a pill for a condition he defends as normal. But if you want an essay in introspective defensiveness and self-contradiction, follow these thoughts of Michael from Essex:

'I hope you will give your sympathetic attention to what will inevitably be a long-winded letter, as I feel inhibited about talking on one of your radio phone-ins.

My problem is doubtless familiar to you – middle-aged lack of virility, or worse, the fear of it. I will try to put down everything which might be of relevance and therefore will surely include much which is inconsequential, but here goes.

Aged 41, married for 10 years to a wife with whom I have a supremely happy relationships in terms of companionship. We are each other's favourite company on holidays, eating out, theatres and social life in general – shared tastes and sense of humour. By common consent we have no children, both of us working and enjoying a measure of independence, and have every intention of staying together.

Now to the problem area. I am aware that there are varying levels of sexuality and have been aware since teenage that I exhibit certain symptoms that might indicate a lowish level. For instance, never at any age had ejaculation travelled more than just beyond the end of the penis; except at times of arousal, the scrotal sac is invariably flaccid; at a relatively early age, early morning erections ceased to occur, except during the first stage of a sexual relationship; relatively long recovery period after intercourse.

Despite all that, I have had (and am still having, but more of that later) extremely satisfactory sex with several women including my wife. She and I had a very physical relationship for about five years before we married, but not very long afterwards she began to lose interest in sex, and without her active co-operation, I began to feel less and less virile, and less inclined to coax her into lovemaking for fear of an embarrassing failure. *How I have envied the stereotype indiscriminately randy totally confident male* [my italics] of whom, perhaps unfortunately, I number several among my close friends.

During those years (say aged 33 onwards) sex at home was at intervals of weeks rather than days, and invariably occurred when I had been drinking enough to obliterate any self-consciousness. At the same time, with a conviction that I was prematurely ageing in the sexual department, I actually passed up chances of affairs with at least one highly attractive woman because of this anxiety. Here is a contradiction which I can only set down for what it is worth; during those years, I did have highly satisfactory sex with two women over a period of 36 months each. The sexual encounters in both cases tended to be spaced out in terms of several weeks. In both cases, before the affairs gently faded to a very friendly conclusion, with each lady finding a more permanently available partner, I was becoming aware of the problem that as the initial ardour wore off, the damn thing was exhibiting a reluctance to stand up.

This takes me to the late 70s or thereabouts and a time when I really thought my sex-life was over, my wife being by now totally uninterested in bed, though still a cheerful, amusing and devoted companion. Then out of the blue (1979) I met another woman. To my utter astonishment she was, and is, able to make me perform like 20 all over again, and has convinced me that, in spite of everything I have told you re physical make-up, a very large part of the problem must surely lie in the mind.

I was quite careless about my wife discovering the start of the affair, and it was a very real surprise when she made the most tremendous fuss, threatening divorce. I told her very firmly that this was purest dog-in-the-manger attitude and that while I had no desire to leave home, I wasn't going to miss the chance of re-discovering my sexuality when it didn't interfere with our life together. I should explain that we both spend a fair amount of time away from home. This had the effect of dramatically improving our sex-life for some time, but, here we go again, now that the initial excitement of my affair is abating slightly (e.g. morning tumescence no longer regularly in evidence) I have recently failed with my wife three times in succession. This is despite the fact that though never randy she is nowadays extremely sympathetic. The most recent episode which has sparked off this letter happened this morning and is typical. By the time it has taken gently to awaken her, my erection has disappeared – not to worry, both very sleepy. Quietly cuddling and erect again perhaps half an hour later, but gone in the time it takes to think "Fine, let's try again". My wife tries to encourage me with kisses, and not in any perfunctory way either, but with much tenderness. Penis does its utmost to shrink back inside my body. I ask her to desist. She does so without resentment, without even disappointment.

So what, I ask myself, is the problem?

Well, I think love-making is important, apart from which I revel in the feeling of my own maleness when I can catch the elusiveness of it. Surely, I should be able to summon up the wherewithal to make love in a spirit of togetherness and tenderness, without needing the stimulus of the start of an affair?

I have certainly bent your ear pretty thoroughly, haven't I? I feel that you just might be able to help and I look forward to hearing from you.

P.S. I know that I have indicated clearly that the virility problem is not of fundamental importance to the continuation of my marriage, but it most definitely is vital to my happiness of mind.'

I can only hope that by this stage Michael has received the message of the present chapter, namely that the penis is inherently unreliable as an instrument of male assertion and will always refuse to perform a ritual war dance.

6 Work Kills – Official

'Men have two basic needs. Neither of them, no matter what they say, is sex. They need love and they need work. And work takes priority over love. If a woman could know only one fact about men and work it should be that work is the most seductive mistress most men ever have' (Dr Joyce Brothers, *What Every Woman Should Know About Men*, 1981)

'Three per cent of the British workforce now works in agriculture which supplies 60 per cent of our food needs ... the entire British demand for TVs and video cassette recorders ... could be supplied by a couple of super-efficient factories in Japan. One microchip plant in Malaysia employing 400 people can supply the entire worldwide demand for a certain type of electronic device. There simply isn't going to be the large number of "jobs" in the traditional sense any more' (*New Society*, 14/9/1983)

'I think every chap feels that when he's laid off, why me? It's my job that's been pushed to one side and you're sort of thrown on the scrap heap.' (Tony Mason, unemployed, *Men . . .*, BBC2, 1984)

'All days were work days. "There weren't any hours with him; there weren't any days of the week." The days did not include breaks, coffee or otherwise ... he had worked so feverishly, driven himself so furiously, forced his young will to be inflexible ... He had tried to do everything – everything – possible to succeed, to earn respect, to "be somebody"' (Robert A. Caro, *The Years of Lyndon Johnson – The Path to Power*, 1982)

Men's relationship with work is complex. They need it in order to survive and yet it can destroy them. I have already noted in Chapter 1 that being *out* of work can seriously damage your health. An American study covering a 34-year period, for example, estimated that every one per cent on the unemployment rate added just over four per cent to the suicide rate, exactly four per cent to the admission rate to State prisons, five per cent to the murder rate, about three per cent to mental hospital admissions, and almost two per cent to the death rate generally. In the UK the men most at risk from the mental strains of unemployment are middle-aged and working class.

However, being *in* work can also endanger your health and the effects are by no means confined to senior manual labourers. All age groups and social classes of British men are afflicted by work stress. While it is true that industrial accidents are uncommon in the plastic environments of Head Offices, here both executive and clerical personnel are exceptionally vulnerable to sedentary conditions such as heart attacks, hardening of the arteries and high blood pressure. When we recall that men live on average between seven and eight years less than women and are less able than women to cope with life stress, it is natural to conclude that it is probably their comprehensive commitment to work that kills them off. Accordingly, the work god must have a lot going for him if men are ready to offer themselves up as human sacrifices. They certainly insist on being labelled as paid-up believers.

As noted in Chapter 1, men continue to define themselves in terms of their job at a time when work itself is in short supply. This has obviously faced many traditional supporters of the work ethic with an existential and not just an economic problem. If such a man is hit by unemployment and cannot find a new role in life he is confronted with loss of both working faith and identity. The tendency to look back at what you *were* rather than forward to what you *could be* is common:

> '. . . coming down here [to the pub] and sitting with the lads and having a chat and a drink, is the only thing I've got left. Apart from . . . I mean no disrespect to my wife . . . I mean I love her more than owt, you know what I mean. But when all's said and done, this is the last remnant of my life up to getting made redundant that I've got left.' (Vic Green, redundant steel worker, *Men . . .*, BBC2, 1984).

As I have already argued, he must be helped to see that an alternative source of personal identity is already on hand in the network of intimate relationships we share with family and friends.

Concentrating for the moment on male traditionalists *in* work, it is noticeable that there is even an important division made between the masculine content of jobs requiring brawn and jobs requiring brain. The sociologist Paul Willis points out in his study of 'Why working class kids get working class jobs' (*Learning To Labour*, 1977) that *machismo* status is the bait attached to heavy manual work to ensure that proletarian males will grow up wanting to undertake its intrinsic unpleasantness. The manual world seems to offer exciting masculine values to the Tarzans of the shop floor who deride desk-based workers for their supposed effeminacy.

Class apart, all men pay a high price for fulfilling what they variously see as their chosen masculine role. At every level of society, traditionally minded workers discipline themselves to defer gratifications. Talk to a bank manager or a dog-handler and he'll probably get around to telling you he does it 'for the sake of the wife and the kids', yet holding a job means not spending much time *seeing* the wife and the kids. Once work took place in and around the home, but since the Industrial Revolution, paid work has usually entailed men's absence from home, and a sharp split between their working and domestic lives. Some men find this deferral of gratification almost addictive. Their work is a kind of drug. On the face of things, to live for your work may seem admirable. To die for it, however, as Malcolm Carruthers says in *The Western Way of Death* (1974), seems both unnecessary and uneconomic. Those specially at risk are the unsuccessful strivers; and stress-induced coronaries are now becoming just as common among blue collar workers as they are among executives.

To add to men's difficulties, there are now over nine million women also in paid work, who no longer defer to males as exclusive breadwinners. The very reason why some men work – to provide for a wife and children at home – is contradicted by the determination of some wives to earn that living for themselves. Talk to at least seven of the current branch managers of the National Westminster Bank and you will find that they *are* women. The pace and force of female advance has shaken the foundations of patriarchy; this side of World War III, it will never be the same again. Women are demanding a share in the social power conferred on individuals in their role as remunerated workers and in the face of this demand, men can no longer regard themselves as the prescriptive working sex. Many men feel personally intimidated by the new working strength of women. Others regard this as a significant and long-awaited time of choice. Perhaps this is the moment to shrug off the hereditary role and make a purpose in life for oneself outside the world of work?

Such a revolution would yield immediate benefits and not just to men's health and longevity. It would liberate working class youth from self-selected slavery which instead would have to be imposed by external forces – never so easy. Proletarian sexism would wither. If you did not have to be a muscly drudge to be a 'real' man, you might attempt work involving mental tasks more appropriate to our electronic future. The work done by women would thereby appreciate in value, and the gulf-like distinction between work and home might be bridged. With men's participation, the status of domestic tasks might also rise. Working class lads would no longer seek only to mate with mother-like figures and heart-chilling monologues such as this from 'Spike' would no longer be heard:

"'. . . I've got the right bird, I've been goin' with her for eighteen months now. Her's as good as gold. She wouldn't look at another chap. She's fucking done well, she's clean. She loves doing fucking housework. Trousers I brought yesterday, I took 'em up last night, and her turned 'em up for me . . . She's as good as gold and I wanna get married as soon as I can'" (quoted by Willis, 1977).

These revolutionary benefits would not be confined to labouring males since they would necessarily impinge on the 'masculinity' of men throughout society. In any case, the experiences men hold in common far outweigh class contradictions, as we have seen in Chapter 2. The emotional development of *all* boys is governed by precisely held biological beliefs and emotional assumptions on the part of *all* parents. In relation to work, these boil down to a commandment to each burgeoning male that he must 'amount to something' in the world. Boys are instructed from birth that you can only be somebody if you make external achievements which accredit you with power, financial or social. The corollary to this is that you cannot amount to anything in yourself, indeed you are not a *person* unless you have influence over some portion of the world at large. Life is presented as a competitive contest, with you set against the rest. It may be prudent from time to time to form alliances to advance your interests, thus engaging in teamwork, but in the last analysis a successful 'winner' plays his emotional cards very close to his chest. First he is told his emotions are unimportant, since only the world outside is real. Secondly, he is taught to keep them to himself since one of the prudential rules of the adult game of work is to give no person a hold over you.

If the male world is indeed a "war of all against all', in the phrase of Thomas Hobbes, then man's life is solitary, poor, nasty and brutish, as well as being short. The command to compete for a very limited body of prizes is also the command for the majority to fail, and to feel that sense of failure keenly. In a society where only one man can be Leviathan, depression is the order for the rest. Even before you get to this stage, you have to negotiate the injunction that you *are* a nobody. Let us examine a specific historical case. How does it feel to be so emotionally without hope that you imagine everyone is laughing at you for being nothing but yourself? This was the instructive experience of the young Lyndon Johnson, for instance, who suffered right from birth with a cosmic sense of inferiority and insecurity. All his life, he sought external compensations in the form of attention, sympathy, respect and, ultimately, dominance because it was the general view in his home town that 'Lyndon will never amount to anything', a view that his own anxieties had helped to spread.

Yet what else can a man think when trapped within the masculine stereotype? If feelings of insecurity are inadmissible, if no one will accept your right to be both male *and* frail, what alternative has the energetic Bonapartist in this world but to reach up and seize power? It's the obvious salve:

'The more one thus follows [Johnson's] life, the more apparent it becomes that alongside the thread of achievement running through it runs another thread, as dark as the other is bright, and as fraught with consequences for history: a hunger for power in its most naked form, for power not to improve the lives of others, but to manipulate and dominate them, to bend them to his will. For the more one learns – from his family, his childhood playmates, his college classmates, his first assistants, his congressional colleagues – about Lyndon Johnson, the more it becomes apparent not only that this hunger was a constant throughout his life but that it was a hunger so fierce and consuming that no consideration of morality or ethics, no cost to himself – or to anyone else – could stand before it.' (Robert A. Caro, *The Years of Lyndon Johnson*, 1982).

Fortunately for him (if not the world) Johnson was stalwart enough to achieve the position of Leviathan-in-Chief by becoming President of the United States of America. He could even manipulate strong-minded rivals into positions of subordination. Allies who owed their advancement to him, even tough guys like Jesse Kellam, were regularly reduced to tears by displays of Johnsonian brow-beating. All must bow the knee. His wife, 'Lady Bird' Johnson, born to wealth and style, was treated like a skivvy, particularly at socially important parties:

'"Lady Bird, go get me another piece of pie."
"I will, in just a minute, Lyndon."
"*Go get me another piece of pie!*"' (Caro, 1982).

All the time, in the background, one can hear Johnson's inner voice telling him to be somebody because a man who does not command is a nobody:

'. . . he didn't know what he wanted to be, but he wanted to be somebody . . . he couldn't stand not being somebody – just could not *stand* it . . . I felt sorry for him' (Estelle Harbin, former colleague, quoted by Caro, 1982).

Finally, one of his favourite and literally most revealing behaviours was to conduct political business while seated on the toilet. Each morning, fastidious aides would be compelled to take dictation precisely at the moment when nature was also on call.

It's hardly original to say there has to be a better way. All work and no play makes Jack a dull ole boy. Few men, however, stop to consider the essential confidence trick on which the system is based, for the truth is that power in the world doesn't bring you security. The work ethic by itself cannot turn you into a lasting 'somebody'. And many of the alleged 'rewards' for deferring gratification will remain just that – alleged. Quite simply, men usually feel *more* vulnerable when they've risen towards the top because they have more to lose and there are more people trying to take it away from them. Both Johnson (and later President Nixon) progressed from electoral landslide to disgrace within four years. You *never* really get to feel better by trying to reinforce your ego with worldly symbols of success unless you also make yourself vulnerable to love and attachment, qualities of softness which can also topple you from power and so you cannot afford them. Q.E.D. For example, the famous Congressional Speaker, Sam Rayburn, was instructed by his farming father upon leaving home to play it straight and true in that immortal phrase: 'Son, be a man' (Caro, 1982). Rayburn took this to mean he must be honest, truthful and acquire power. He was and he did. 'I've always wanted responsibility because I want the power responsibility brings' he once told the Texas House of Representatives. Later, having acquired power in the Capitol, 'he learned that even power could not save him from what he dreaded . . . the loneliness that consumes people'. He was afraid to get close to men or women. He was mortified with shyness because he had never dared to acquire any intimate social skills. And he was at a loss during the evenings and weekends because work was his entire perspective. An aide summed him up thus:

> 'He had many worshippers, but very few close friends. You held him in awe. You didn't dare get close to him. People feared to get close to him, because they were afraid of saying the wrong thing. And because people were afraid to get close to him, he was a very lonely guy. His life was a tragedy. I felt very, very sorry for Sam Rayburn' (Caro, 1982).

But Samuel Rayburn, he was a *real man* . . .

Regardless of his influence, work is always bigger than the individual:

> '"Last year the insurance industry gave a testimonial dinner in my honour", a patient told Dr Jay B. Rohrlich, a psychiatrist who has written about work and love. "They all made speeches about me. But they were not really about me. They were about my work"' (quoted by Dr Joyce Brothers, *What Every Woman Should Know about Men*, 1982).

When a man is ill, a replacement will be found to do his job. When a man dies, the funeral is rarely for the company which employs him, which will live on. If the company ceases to make a profit during the man's lifetime, he will be expended. Freud said: 'Work gives a man a secure place in the portion of reality, in the human community', but Marx had the last, somewhat bitter laugh, pointing out that working men are both alienated and made insecure by the realities of modern capitalism, realities rendered all the more conspicuous at times of economic slump.

In the final analysis, work could almost be described as a form of insanity which specifically afflicts the majority of men. In Japan, researchers found that 80 per cent of the male workers had *never* taken a holiday. Moreover, in a fascinating experiment:

> 'Japanese men were asked whom they would telephone first if there were an earthquake while they were on their way home. Nearly 40 per cent said they would try to reach their boss first. Only nine per cent indicated that they would try to get in touch with their wives' (Brothers, 1982).

US research indicates that more men commit suicide when they are fired than when their wife or child dies. This would not, in passing, seem to be a particularly skilful way of coping with the problem of rejection, but the evidence goes on to reveal that:

> '. . . men don't talk about being fired . . . They can talk about death, illness, divorce, but not this. It is shameful. It is taboo' (Brothers)

and so they pretend that they haven't lost their jobs or repress the inner pain of rejection until they reach the point of being unable to carry on living. Even death is preferable to giving themselves the relief that *expressing* their shock and anxiety would provide.

Is it that work insanity has turned men into unemotional zombies? Dr Fernando Bartolomé, a French business expert, concluded after studying a group of American executives that what many outsiders had always suspected is true. These men:

> '. . . were not what he called human beings, nor did their world have a human dimension. Not that he saw them as science fiction computeroids, simply as people lacking the ability to show warmth or sadness or even delight.
> They had schooled themselves never to feel dependent on another person. Thirty-six of the forty insisted that they hardly ever felt dependent. Thirty-two of them said that when they did, they would not let anyone know they felt that way.

"Feelings of dependence", said one man, "are signs of weakness." As for showing warmth or affection, forget it. One man said that he had been terribly embarrassed at a dinner party when his wife described another man as being his best friend. It was true, but it was something he preferred to keep to himself. He did not want anyone thinking of him as a man who needed friends' (Brothers, 1982).

Thus it is that little boys who learn the value of working together to win evolve into taciturn men who apply these teamwork lessons only in order to get the other guy fired first. If women are good at picking up the psychological cues at home, men are brilliant at sensing the nuances which determine the fate of their careers in relation to other men at work. The male sex is suffering from morbid compulsions to carry out its chosen role *as a result of* the way in which that role has been defined. In the following pages, evidence of this will be offered in more detail, focusing on the problems of the increasing 'burnout' of the modern business executive, a problem facing all western countries.

The symptoms commence with a subtle allergy to work. Breakfast is dawdled over. Appointments are not kept. The clock is watched. Men rush home at five to grab a life-giving glass of scotch. And another. They experience up to four of the following symptoms: palpitations, low back pain, excess sweating, breathlessness, skin rashes, insomnia, indigestion, piles, coffee addiction, the constant desire to urinate and compulsive eating. Their marriage comes under stress. They have sexual difficulties. They end up staring at the four walls wondering what the hell they've achieved in life. They spend more and more time at work doing less and less. They are usually aged between 30 and 45, with family ties and a responsible position. This is the condition of extreme stress, of a mental burnout.

One gloomy prophet, Dr Sidney Lecker of the Stress Control Center in New York, claims that between one third and a half of all US executives now have their careers damaged by the burnout syndrome. He says the scale of modern business technology has grown to a point where the fallible male body has no place. Only a machine can really cope with the demands of the system. Who else can be on call 24 hours a day, refuel in midflight, ignore domestic ties and contemplate redundancy with imperturbability? In the remaining part of the 20th century, a man can be 'over the hill' in his late 20s. If he's going to make a contribution, particularly in the micro-chip and computer industries, he must do it while still 'young'. In productive terms, his life expectancy has been reduced to that of a mediaeval peasant.

Dr Lecker has a vested interest in spreading doom and despondency, but look at what is happening in all the advanced economies. Lack of employment has increased the competition for existing jobs. Companies blithely expect their surviving employees to give them an arm and a leg for loyalty. Graduates queue up to fill the shoes of any who remain uncooperative. In the recent US Air Traffic Controllers' strike, for example, the trade union complained that too much job stress was putting airline safety at risk since their members were suffering 'burnout'. Shorter hours and better working conditions were therefore demanded. The US Government responded with mass sackings and many thousands of able but less experienced volunteers took the vacant places. In the short term, job stress has actually been increased, not diminished.

Look, too, at what is happening as British companies are being slimmed down. One of the research interviews I carried out when preparing this book was conducted in the previously prosperous light industrial zone of Southall, Middlesex. My contact said the engineering company he worked for had been rationalised to such an extent that they could no longer muster II men for the annual cricket match. His job at least was safe but several close colleagues had been made to bite the bullet of unemployment. Their work did not disappear, since much was vital to the running of the company, it simply piled up on his desk. There is no extra cash for salary increases. If he decided to resign because of this intolerable state of affairs, the company would say 'go ahead'. Almost anyone is easy to replace nowadays and resignation in his case would mean losing 15 years' accumulated severance benefits. He is trapped on the treadmill of the nation's rising 'productivity', although this will do nothing to improve his mental or physical efficiency. Over-worked men only grow tired and careless.

The behavioural psychologist Dr Robert Sharpe says the problem in Britain is now acute: 'Executive burnout is one of the commonest causes of hypertension and infarction. It can be a killer.' He spends a great deal of his time helping commercial high-fliers avoid or recover from the effects of burnout. 'Too many workaholic men', he says, 'get themselves into a situation where they cease to be problem-solving executives, but simply worry about how much there is on their plates. The common factor is that these are people who don't allocate energy very well. Nor do they realise that age takes its toll. At 36, a man has fewer units of psychic energy available to do his job than at 26. He must count these units and when they are spent, he must rest. The alternative is an overload.

'Take three typical examples of burnout. The first is a late 30s male. He may have an "existential" problem. He's got a wife and two kids but they don't appreciate him. On the other hand, he has rows with his wife morning, noon and night and only pats his kids on the head once a day if he remembers, so he isn't entitled to very much affection. But he has a constant complaint on his mind: "What's it all been for . . . what's been in it for me?"

'Now that his wife has decided she wants an interesting job or, worse still, a lover, he feels completely threatened and displaced. There is a net disparity between the 20 years' haul of hard work he's put in and the reward he gets – the personal pay-off. He not unnaturally shows signs of demotivation and fatigue. This is not what his parents promised when he first went to college. They said if he succeeded in business, everything else – family, social and leisure life – would fall into place. Instead he feels completely cheated. He's a high risk candidate for burnout as is any man suffering from this sense of unjust recompense from the masculine stereotype' says Dr Sharpe.

'The second common case is the man who can never say no. He gets overpromoted because he can't turn a job down even when he knows it will prove exhausting. All his other colleagues load him up with their dirty work and he always takes it on. He is the backbone of many enterprises. By training often an accountant or auditor, he rapidly becomes overall traffic manager of the things that go wrong which nobody else wants to put right. He is in obvious danger of suffering a straightforward breakdown variant of burnout.

'The third typical candidate is the guy who can't let go. He is an obsessional perfectionist, often the owner of his own company, who never delegates a single piece of paper or 'phone call. As soon as the business became successful, he should have kicked himself upstairs and let the troops get on with it, but he won't. Or rather, he can't. He even prowls round the building at midnight peering into the files for evidence of disloyalty and counting the paperclips for proof of waste. Alas, this is the greatest possible abuse of his own time and energy. This man will be shaken rigid to find himself one morning lying in the Harley Street Clinic recovering from a premature heart attack, or visiting my consulting rooms to discover just how to come to terms with his neurotic and self-destructive behaviour.'

In Sharpe's view, these three men likely to suffer burnout — the demotivated executive, the 'spaniel' who can't say no and the supremo who can't let go — are all directed to inappropriate masculine/workaholic goals. The first candidate thinks work success will make him lovable — 'My wife will realise I love her because I give her lots of housekeeping, and then she will love me'. But this doesn't happen. The second candidate believes everyone will admire him for being the world's most wonderful coper — 'They'll always need me if I never let them down', but the day he enters hospital, a new dogsbody will step forward. The third imagines his employees dote on him with respect — 'They know my finger's on every pulse and that I make everything happen around here', but the workforce actually regards him as an interfering old bastard.

'Ultimately', says Sharpe, 'all these businessmen reach a point of schedule strain. They can't get through the mass of work in the time available. Therefore, instead of tackling tasks on a day-to-day basis as before, they lapse into worry. They get personally stuck. They can't hack it. They spend time staring stupidly into space like rabbits caught in a headlight. They begin to have trouble sleeping. They feed themselves with negative self-talk. Instead of saying "The auditors are coming and we're two hundred thousand quid off target, how do we dress it up?" they call themselves a failure and lapse into depression.

'Of course, depression is part of the human condition but most of us find a way to feel reinforced by the environment (with money, power, love etc.). But executives crack up when these reinforcers no longer work. For example, the depressed business manager who finds that £50,000 a year does not solve all his problems (and did nothing to stop his wife running off with a student drop-out) will not be comforted by getting a £10,000 a year increase.' Power and money can't buy you love, but you'd be surprised, says Sharpe, how many executives need to find this out the hard way.

Why is this? How did our auto-destructive trio ever get misdirected to 'inappropriate goals' in the first place? The answers lie in our childhood. All these men want to be liked but suffer from the delusion that only successful supermen are likeable. Nothing in their upbringing taught them that it is safe to show vulnerability or fragility. Mum and Dad only praised 'winners' or proved by their own example that normal adults are armour-plated. Another expert in this area, the psychologist Dr Paul Brown of Frederick Chusid and Co. in London, spends his life-time showing executives that their most stressful and costly business errors may be traced back to their relationship with their parents. 'We are all at risk of regarding the company which employs us as a father or a mother', says Brown. 'Woe betide the company hiring an executive who is still in subconscious rebellion against parental authority . . . and woe betide the executive.'

If these are the questions concerning workaholic burnout, what are the answers? Can you, for instance, be your own fire brigade? Most men need to start by understanding stress. 'Every human system and every sub-system must alternate between tension and relaxation, if it is to be efficient, if it is to grow, in fact if it is to survive', says yet another psychology expert, Dr Brendan McGann. 'The ultimate survival skill is learning the importance of doing nothing.' Tension is necessary to life – without it there can be no behaviour. It is not tension that kills us, it is *continual tension without relief*.

The reason lies in the neurology of the human body. We possess a two-stage, self-regulating system. The 'sympathetic' part gears us for action, copes with crises, primes our muscles for 'fight or flight' and fills our blood with adrenalin. By contrast, the 'parasympathetic' nervous system takes care of 'rest and digestion', repair and recreation – in a word, relaxation. It is there to cancel out the effects of crisis management. Unfortunately, and here's the catch, it takes twice as long to get into operation as the sympathetic system and works at its best when there is least interruption, usually when you are asleep. Hands up those managers who realise that for every hour spent on the job under duress they must take nearly two hours off doing nothing (preferably sleeping) in order to maintain a routine level of human efficiency? And relax is the one thing highly stressed businessmen say they can never do?

One reason for this is that, as I noted earlier in this chapter, tension is addictive. You get an adrenalin buzz out of being stressed, although in the long term it builds up greater fatigue. Another is that stress can be masked for several weeks by the stimulants alcohol, coffee and nicotine. These drugs tend to increase your cortisone production so that the body is able to endure higher levels of stress overload. But if you remain in that condition, a sort of permanent 'red alert', the organism will break down at its weakest points, i.e. the spinal discs, the digestion, the sexual system. So how can you survive a modern executive life-style?

One excellent way of coping with quite a severe degree of stress is by taking exercise. This, after all, is nature's way of balancing the books. The man playing a fierce game of squash (see Chapter 7) creates 'parallel stress' together with all the signs of furious anger (red face, sweat, racing pulse). After the combat (not played to the death!), he is too tired to remain tense, too tired to be angry, too tired to care, so the tension is burned off till next time; the parasympathetic nervous system then brings him natural release. He may even return to his desk and fall asleep. Exercise creates some stress by adding to physical fatigue and demanding its own form of disciplined concentration, but it automatically clears the mind of that nagging sense of personal, mental frustration.

Better still is sex, which actually creates a mood of transition from work to play and in many cases allows you to drift into the most restorative of post-coital naps. However, many stressed executives find they cannot even make the first transition from the 'working mode' to the 'arousal mode'. They are fatigued and depressed by the events of the day and so are their libidos, which is why an awful lot of whisky gets consumed at around six o'clock when love-making would be medically preferable.

The first step to a healthy life is thus to learn how to make a safe transition out of the working mode itself. This is what is meant by 'relaxation'. The key is being able to sit still and do nothing. If you are one of those people who can't bear to lie on a beach for more than five minutes, then it's to you that doctors are talking. Put your excess energy into enforced horizontality. Glue your backside to the sofa, empty your head, flex and then relax every muscle in turn and do this for at least half an hour each evening. You will then be amazed to discover that you can make love with your wife or girlfriend if you want to. Your body will obey you. You will also be able to pursue any alternative hobby with real interest instead of feeling like a robot. You will even be able to avoid the telly trap (it is actually intensely stressful to focus your eyes on the TV screen) and at the end of the day you will be able to go to sleep without pills.

The next important task is to take a personal audit. Learning how to do nothing, says Dr Sharpe, although valuable, will not improve your life skills. It will not, for instance, make your irascible boss go away. So you have to do some internal account-ing. What are your strengths and weaknesses when it comes to relationships at home and at work? Do you really know what your realistic targets are? Is promotion feasible or will it cost too much effort? Are you bad at negotiating what you want from your superiors and subordinates? Do you need to develop new skills in relation to those colleagues who seem to be more successful than you? Are there some problems that always cause rows? Is there a special danger time of day when you are usually feeling bloody-minded? And how about the people in your domestic life, for example your wife? Is jealousy a problem? A little self-knowledge will go a long way in helping you get new reactions from other people. If the shop steward always gets up your nose when you're hungry at 12.51, either avoid him or pretend he's your best friend so that his behaviour *has* to change to adapt to yours. You have nothing to lose except a prime source of aggro.

If you succeed in making office life happier, it's likely you could earn further breaks. Perhaps you'll stop driving home like a maniac (which can send your pulse soaring from 65 to 200 beats/minute out of pure stress) just because you hate everyone who stands between you and domestic sanctuary. You might consider taking a walk at lunch-time to relieve the morning's tensions rather than overeating and drinking in an attempt to hide the symptoms. Anything is possible if you start to steer a course *out* of the firing line.

Of course, the over-riding problem is your own personal ambition. Can you be realistic about your power-drive? If this has warped your life, is it perhaps time to re-orientate? If you are already 44 and unlikely ever to become the Chairman, why not settle for what *is* possible? After all, it's not even really true in America that *any* man can become President. Accordingly, the latest research from that country shows that a few of the youngest crop of today's executives are beginning to re-think their priorities. Psychologist and career specialist Dr Brown says unheard of things are happening. One or two new executives are not being tempted by high cash bonuses. Some men refuse (like Britain's Dr David Owen) to be parted from their families at weekends. A handful of young diplomats are not agreeing to un-wanted postings, such as Beirut and Baghdad, which would 'advance their careers'.

'. . . they're going much more for "quality-of-life" arguments than simply "striving" arguments. So men will not move at the organisation's demand if the family is settled, the kids are happy at school and the wife is in the kind of job she wants. Fifteen years ago that was an unthinkable decision. Men moved.' (*Men* . . ., BBC2, 1984).

Men have seen what happens to the older generation, they understand that every man has his burnout point and they believe the game is honestly not worth the candle. Dead men make no sales. Work kills: official.

7 Fight Aggression – Play Squash

'We need men who love a fight, who when they get up in the morning spit on their hands and ask "Whom will I kill today?"' (Eric Hoffer, quoted by Tavris and Offir, *The Longest War: Sex Differences in Perspective*, 1977)

'War is man's work ... biological convergence on the battlefield would not only be dissatisfying in terms of what women could do, but it would be an enormous psychological distraction for the male who wants to think that he is fighting for that woman somewhere behind, not up there in the same foxhole with him. It tramples the male ego. When you get right down to it, you've got to protect the manliness of war' (General Robert H. Barrow, Commandant of the US Marines, *New Society*, 28/7/1983)

'In every society in which men and women differ in aggressiveness, men are the more aggressive' (Maccoby and Jacklin, *The Psychology of Sex Differences*, 1974)

'Elizabeth Senecal of Orlando, Florida, tried to stop her husband watching TV football. He vented his irritation by killing her with a single karate chop' (*Daily Mail*)

'When I lose it's like a knife wound in the stomach' (Former world squash champion Jonah Barrington, *Observer*, 10/2/1980)

The male chauvinist empire has made victims of both the sexes, trapping women in menial roles and men in masterful ones. Nowhere is this made more clear than in the field of employment. More than 40 per cent of the British workforce is female but women are concentrated in occupations officially classified as 'women's work' – the service and 'caring' professions, teaching and typing. They receive lower pay and have worse conditions than men. Few women have yet been allowed into top positions, even in their own fields, although many are well qualified and many more still would welcome the opportunity to rise up the ladder. But higher up the ladder sit all those men.

Over 95 per cent of architects, engineers, scientists and solicitors are men; more than 98 per cent of university professors are men; and some 88 per cent of all medical consultants are men. And these men feel *obliged* to be where they are. In effect, it has been a male compulsion to push the 'Peter Principle' to its ultimate absurdity: that is to say, tens of thousands of men have eagerly risen to their natural level of incompetence. Since the biological distribution of intelligence and talent is *equal* between the sexes, to draw some 90 per cent of your senior social personnel from only *one* sex betokens illogic and superstition: the superstition of 'man's duty to be boss'.

I say that men feel 'obliged' to get to the top, but it is sometimes unfair to characterise their devotion to duty as 'eager'. Many men are crushed by the pressures of the rat race and others would willingly resign tomorrow if someone could demonstrate that it is acceptably masculine to give up. This is particularly true of those men who know they have been promoted beyond the reach of their abilities. In the case of managers in British industry, for example, where at least 80 per cent of middle ranking executives have received no management training of any kind, the feeling is commonplace.

Thus the past order of male social dominance has discomfited both sexes. All armies have shot men for cowardice, for behaving 'like women' when the least attractive option was to behave 'like a man'. The threat of the death penalty is one of the most blatant means of exercising social control. But other, rather more subtle, methods are equally effective in depriving both sexes of their social freedom.

Men have been trained to feel so hostile to feminine things in general (and so to define many hostile things as feminine) that they are well and truly snared in their own delusion. For example, it is instructive to notice just how far men have been taught that the language of efficient personal abuse is speech scornful of women and their works. We all know about the four-letter words, about the *c* . . . a man will be called for offending a male van driver in any one of a hundred different motoring confrontations (if he stops for a child at a pedestrian crossing, for instance). How can a man get in touch with the female side of himself under these circumstances? Men, as we know, are not supposed to cry, whatever the fashion on the women's page of the *Guardian*. Water drops remain women's weapons. Therefore, men have no successful means of coping with situations which make them want to cry. They have to get angry with themselves for even feeling like they want to cry. Once they achieve anger, the emotion is all too often externalised and deflected onto the shoulders of a woman. This is a dreadful waste of men's mental energy and a cruel abuse of the relationship between the sexes.

In the masculine stereotype, real men are not supposed to show anxiety of any kind; that is what girls and babies do. After years of conditioning, 'proper' men automatically convert pain into aggression. In order to be men at all we have to do this so that we may be distinguished from the so-called 'weaker' sex. Nature is called in to assist:

> '. . . dozens of studies show that males of all ages engage in more physical aggression, verbal aggression and play aggression than females do. The difference shows up as soon as children begin to play with each other, at the age of two or three, and lasts into adulthood' (Tavris and Offir, *The Longest War: Sex Differences In Perspective*, 1977).

As discussed in Chapter 3, there is a hot dispute concerning whether males are more aggressive because of their hormones or because parents positively encourage boys to be stroppy, but whatever the reason, men today have certain elemental behavioural tendencies towards belligerence at the individual level. The same is true, as Konrad Lorenz has shown, of their group behaviour:

> 'Every man of normally strong emotions knows, from his own experience, the subjective phenomena that go hand in hand with the response of militant enthusiasm. A shiver runs down the back and, as more exact observation shows, along the outside of both arms. One soars, elated, above all the ties of everyday life, one is ready to abandon all for the call of what, in the moment of this specific emotion, seems to be a sacred duty. All obstacles in its path become unimportant; the instinctive inhibitions against hurting or

killing one's fellows lose, unfortunately, much of their power. Rational considerations, criticism, and all reasonable arguments against the behaviour dictated by militant enthusiasms are silenced by an amazing reversal of values, making them appear not only untenable but base and dishonourable. Men may enjoy the feeling of absolute righteousness even while they commit atrocities ...' (*On Aggression*, 1966).

This amazing 'reversal of values', both social and personal, amounts to a 'burden of aggressive dominance' for men which on the whole they are poorly adapted to cope with.

Why is it thought to be so essential for men to shoulder this burden? After all, we are all born with the same high levels of personal anxiety. Male infants cry just as quickly as females when their mothers leave the room. In any case, male aggression, whether learned or innate, is no longer vital to well populated, modern societies committed to peace and the pursuit of high technology. They no longer regard world war as an affordable option and usually prefer survival to showdowns. In fact, the primeval concept of 'militant enthusiasm' as described by Konrad Lorenz above is no longer even admired (witness the world's incredulity at the Iranian revival of the self-sacrificial 'Holy War'). It is viewed in the same light as male hooliganism on the streets or at football parks. Similarly the tendency to take the law into your own hands should your patriarchal authority be challenged is no longer accepted. Today, if you hit the man who 'insults' your wife or sleeps with your daughter the offence is yours and not his.

Finally, as we have seen in Chapter 6 and will shortly discuss in relation to driving, males are inadequately equipped by heredity and culture to absorb the stress of an aggressive posture. It doesn't take much common sense to see that if all provocations lead to confrontations which tend to get out of hand, and men can only reply in the voice of anger to all personal challenges, then men will soon fall victim to nervous exhaustion.

For all these reasons, aggression is in effect the very last thing men need to cultivate. Fortunately, there appears to be a growing consensus that, in the words of one philosopher:

'... given a certain genetic constitution, and within the bounds of that endowment, whatever man is he learns to be, especially in respect to values, morality and customs

... man has acquired responsibilities that he did not recognise before' (J. R. Munson, Professor of Philosophy, University of Missouri).

So even if a man cannot choose whether or not to feel aggressive, he certainly can choose how to express that aggression and whether or not to esteem violence as innately masculine or dismiss gentleness as inherently feminine. (A parallel argument for women might run: just because many women cannot choose whether or not to suffer from pre-menstrual tension, it doesn't mean they are compelled by that temporary burst of depression to murder their husbands and lovers.) This can be stated even more strongly. If men have found it possible to undervalue their gentle feelings by means of self and social conditioning, why do they imagine it would be so difficult to undervalue their aggressive feelings? If they started to lift their repressions they would rarely need to resort to their aggressions to deflect emotional pain: they could talk and weep instead.

Thus, if there is indeed truth in the rumour that men are too habituated to violence to reform in a hurry, at least they can attempt to channel this aggression into safer conduits by placing more emphasis on symbolic struggles. Even if we took the most cynical view of masculine nature, and suggested that the problem of male hooliganism, vandalism and domestic violence is due to the fact that: 'we haven't had a good European war for such a long time', it would help if men made an effort to acknowledge that it is adequately masculine merely to 'play' at being aggressive.

This argument would carry more weight with men if only they would realise that fighting *for real* is an incompetent and dangerous way to achieve their targets. By way of illustration (and leaving aside world war), let us spend the remainder of this chapter comparing the incompetent and dangerous uses to which men put the 'game' of motor bike and car driving with the sensible but every bit as satisfying symbolic aggressiveness of the game of squash.

The majority of motor bikes in this country are ridden by fairly competitive young men with the result that of the 947 male rider fatalities that occurred in 1981, 863 of the victims were aged between 16 and 39 (and 760 between 17 and 29). In the same period, of the 1125 of male car drivers who met their deaths on the road, some 629 were aged between 16 and 39 (and 427 between 17 and 29). As many as 64 per cent of all rider/driver deaths on the road occur to men in this age range (see Table I).

Looking beyond the aggressiveness of many of these young men in search of their Manufacturer, we can find an even more telling statistic in the comparison of the death rates for male and female car drivers of all age groups. Whereas only 221 women drivers died on the roads during 1981, a total of 1125 men drivers achieved the same quietus. During the same period, only 37 per cent more men than women applied for driving licences. Even allowing for greater vehicle usage by men than women, we must conclude that men are obviously doing something in cars which

Table I Motor vehicle rider/driver deaths for 1981
(Department of Transport official figures)

Motor cycle riders

Age	Male dead	Female dead
10–14	1	0
15	7	0
16	35	3
17–19	429	13
20–29	331	9
30–39	69	0
40–49	21	5
50–59	22	3
60–69	23	0
70+	10	1
Total	947	34

Car drivers

Age	Male dead	Female dead
16	6	0
17–19	113	17
20–29	314	58
30–39	196	43
40–49	141	20
50–59	131	33
60–69	117	26
70+	107	25
Total	1125	221

Total number of vehicle licence applications in 1981

Men: 833,255	*Women:* 521,160

women are not; and it seems calculated to kill them in greater numbers. If women were as reckless behind the wheel as men, by the law of strict equality there should have been 708 dead female car drivers in 1981, not 221.

Could it be that women have twigged that roads are no place to disport aggressive traits – bearing in mind that a total of 18 people die every single day while using them? For the under-35 age group of males, road accidents are actually the primary cause of death. In Northern Ireland, more men die each year because they travel on the roads than because they are involved in that country's politics. If as many people died each day on the railways, they would be closed down. If a jumbo jet crashed at Heathrow killing all on board every month, nobody would fly. And yet mass murder is apparently permissible on our asphalt surfaces. The motorway madness and in-town grand prix lunacy of principally male drivers engaged in a genuine struggle to the death is apparently OK. Another term for this behaviour is war; another term for it would be psychosis.

Many male motorists are wedded to their wheels in an ego-related, I-must-be-in-control, I'm-in-charge sort of a way. The great outcry against rail disasters is obviously to do with the anonymous threat from a *public* form of transport. If, however, you kill yourself in the privacy of your own tin box, then that's your affair, although so often you take a few innocent people (up to six pedestrians?) with you. The Road Research Laboratory's computer will produce thousands of references in support of the contention that the principal hazard to safe road usage is male aggression. Studies of the 'aggressive', the 'active-aggressive' and the 'passive-aggressive-cum-retaliatory' motorist abound. On the whole, aggressive people choose aggressive cars to be aggressive in.

This may remind you of an advertising campaign once used in Britain for the Fiat motor car. Perhaps it is no coincidence that the land of the Latin lover, the spaghetti western, the *mafioso* and the bottom-pincher produced copy as 'masculine' as the following:

> 'This handsome animal [depicted 'growling' in a cage] is the Supermirafiori, bred in Italy by Fiat. Don't be fooled by its sleek looks . . . Under that beautiful body lurks an angry beast. Turn the key and you'll find out how fierce it is. A 1600 twin cam engine . . . delivers 96 bhp, a top speed of 106 mph and gets from 0–60 in 11.1 secs. Making it an animal that's hard to catch'.

Notice the emphasis on 36 mph of illegal speed and wild

animality, the hunt, the chase, the law of the jungle. Bear in mind that the number of children aged between four and seven killed on Britain's roads could be almost halved by a 10 mph reduction in speed limits on minor urban roads – a reduction which would increase overall journey times by only five per cent. But doubtless that handsome Fiat animal would still be zooming around from 0–60 in 11.1 seconds whatever the speed limit, because that is the bait with which it is sold.

Rolls Royce are little better. Their equivalent 1978 advertising campaign in the *Times* extolled the 'Spirit of Ecstasy' which is what you experience apparently behind the wheel of a Roller. No, you don't stay calm and careful with your mind on the task in hand, you become ecstatic, *over*-emotional, eerily cut off from reality.

Of course, as S. W. Quenault (*Driver Behaviour – Safe and Unsafe Drivers**) shows, it is not just aggressive drivers that are dangerous; for example, some men are hazardous because they are always *timorous* behind the wheel. But general experience (and personal observation on the roads of London) reveals an overall picture of paranoid pugnacity graded by vehicle type. Thus in the capital we have Homo BMW ('racing for *lebensraum*'), Homo Ford Escort Van ('my delivery or your life'), Homo Black Cab ('cutting corners where none exist'), Homo Range Rover ('I can do 110 mph on the inside lane'), Homo Mini Cooper 'S' ('I can do 110 mph on the pavement'), Homo Jaguar ('being vulgar, I leave my car to do a great deal of social climbing for me'), Homo Unladen Articulated Lorry ('yeah, well, I've got a Golf GTI at home and this thing handles well'), Homo Datsun ('pseudo-Kamikaze at a price you can afford'), Homo VW Conversion with Big Tyres ('you think I'm just a beetle – well remember Franz Kafka') – and so on.

Driving seems to bring out the worst in people so that their worst behaviour becomes their standard driving behaviour. If Father blows his top at the sonovabitch who won't get out of the way, Mother and the rest of the family accept it tolerantly. They think that spontaneous driver rage is a perfectly *normal* male phenomenon. But they shouldn't. Anger should not be indulged even in the overtaking lane of an empty motorway when the guy in front is doing a steady 45 mph. The mortality rates explain why.

* All pamphlets on driving supplied by the Transport and Road Research Laboratory, Crowthorne, Berks.

What is it about aggressive driving which makes us men feel so good? For example, why is overtaking always an ego-rewarding behaviour for all but the tiny minority of passive male drivers? Perhaps we have to conclude that millions of men are driving around on our roads in an acute state of inferiority complex.

A more metaphysical theory could be that men not only wish to reach the head of the motorised queue, but to go faster and faster and never stop, to reach vanishing point, kinaesthetic ecstasy. I think we are actually looking for a climax forbidden by the Highway Code, engendered by an automotive machine to which we can never become adapted. For, alas, man cannot blend properly with this machine. For a start, cars with fast acceleration and high top speeds are addictive. The driver actually becomes unstable whilst driving them. The dicing with other road competitors, sudden bursts of motion, grabbing an advantage, all these produce high noradrenalin (the 'kick' hormone) secretions in the human body which take some time to dissipate. And since a driver does not use his muscles to burn off the emotion this produces, his body must absorb the tension and heat. This produces stress, but not of a productive and stimulating variety. N. W. Heimstra (*The Effects Of Stress Fatigue On Performance In A Simulated Driving Situation*) says that 'findings support the concept that stress brings an emotional arousal which may interfere with performance on tasks such as driving'. In other words, the very act of handling a modern car produces biochemical changes in the body which produce an emotional state that may make the driver incompetent to manage his motor. This is far more true for men than women since men routinely respond to stress aggressively, thereby increasing the stress-load. Stressed individuals are much more likely to run their vehicles into you than non-stressed drivers, so beware above all the recently divorced male under threat of redundancy who, on what is possibly his last day behind the wheel of the glittering company Granada, hurtles along behind you up the M1.

And finally, when you consider the fact that 34 per cent of British drivers killed in road accidents recently had alcohol levels above the legal limits, you can begin to see exactly what the modern motor car has helped the traditionally minded male to become – an intoxicated, over-powered killer*. One is forced to

---

* Two other interesting facts concerning the dangerous combination of cars and men have emerged from various road studies. L. Moser (*Die Geschwindigkeit im Strassenverkehr*) notes that:

conclude that wherever possible Mother should take the wheel of the family car out of Father's hands. She is less likely to take it for an ego-drive.

How much better for road safety if male motoring offenders, instead of facing fines, were required to play a bi-weekly game of squash with maximum exertion and minimum quarter. Here is a species of competition aggressive enough for the toughest of Fiat copywriters. It is by no means the perfect answer, since some men get so carried away they play as though their lives depended on winning. Yet as a means of socialising male aggression, of transposing the desire to fight into a symbolic contest, of permitting men to remain 'masculine' without being destructive, of allowing men to discharge their aggressions without killing their fellows in cars or wars, squash is a safer bet.

It provides, as Rex Bellamy of the *Times* puts it, 'unparalleled opportunities for being nasty . . . with unusual scope for the unscrupulous'. For a start, it's not a team game. The struggle is between you and the individual you're trying to smash. Next, since squash offers the world's highest energy expenditure per time allowed of any game, it also offers the world's greatest sense of exhausted elation in victory and knackered anguish in defeat. Thirdly, it is the epitome of a 'man's game', by which I mean no disrespect to the three quarter of a million women players in this country. Brute strength and power make more of a difference between male and female performance at squash than tennis. The World Ladies Champion could be defeated by most of the top men players and many down the ladder too.

It is even fractionally violent. Look at the floor of any squash court and you will see dried blood. You may also be lucky enough to see wet blood. 'Then towards the end of the third game', writes ex-Open Champion Jonah Barrington in *The Book Of Jonah* (Barrington and Everton, 1972), 'Geoff began to tire.

'Physiologic characteristics of the human eye make it impossible for drivers to estimate speeds above 60 kilometres per hour with any accuracy'

and J. MacMillan (*Deviant Drivers*) has found:

'. . . a strong association between deviance and social maladjustment and male motoring convictions',

both adding even more weight to my belief that most modern cars are the last sort of weapon we should place into the hands of any stereotyped human male.

He was also struck by my racket on the backswing . . . The cut that he had on the eye did not affect his vision in any way although the blood that ran down the side of his face. . . .'

Anyone who plays squash will have received a purple-and-red anemone-like bruise somewhere on his body from the ball. It is all part of the game:

> 'Don't hit the ball hard at your opponent if he is getting in the way a bit. Gently will do' (Official Squash Diary).

Taken all in all, the game is bound to cause some trouble since there isn't enough room to stand without pushing. You see, squash has taken the *two* sides of a tennis court and stuck them one on top of the other so that both players are playing on the *same* side of the net, competing in each other's territory not only for ball and shot but for the very space in which to play. As a result, most games of squash resemble the fight for territory of the Ugandan kob (a lusting antelope).

This competitive claustrophobia satisfies the strongest masculine imperatives. Winning is the crisis. The PRO at the Squash Racket Association once told me:

> 'It isn't much of a game apart from the score. In tennis, only a small number of clubs have leagues and ladders – all squash clubs do. The artistry of the stroke is enough at tennis; squash is about victory'.

Jonah Barrington adds:

> 'When I lose it's like a knife wound in the stomach . . . The most vital thing to me in squash is winning'.

He adds that when he was 13 he wanted to be Napoleon, so it isn't really surprising:

> I had a tremendous competitive streak and clearly unsporting nature . . . I never shook hands before a competition'

and I daresay Napoleon never shook hands before a battle either, although Jonah Barrington has not left hundreds of thousands of mothers grieving for their slaughtered sons as did the Emperor of France.

Even the gentle Tommy Steele, singer, fund-raiser and

squash-nut who trains for two hours a day and lives in a squash court attached to his house confesses:

> 'Winning matters enormously. I have to win, though in the Pakistani fashion I try to take, not tear, my opponents to pieces'.

What is the meaning of all this winning? Is the triumph erotically arousing? Is the destruction of a rival male a surrogate sexual experience, yet another outlet for our supposed primordial gaiety? Contemplate the parallels. You start the match by knocking up (foreplay), you toss to see who serves, you choose which position, you pound the sweat out of each other for 40 minutes, then run to the bathroom having achieved climax and compare notes on your performance. Can it be that?

Tommy Steele says he can apply what he has learned from squash to everything else:

> 'When I'm thwarted in show business I say to myself it's no worse than a cross court drive and I know how to deal with them'.

Comic actor Leonard Rossiter also goes this far: he plays squash every day of the week and often goes to a squash village for a vacation because '. . . it helps him to do well in all other things', says Mrs Rossiter. 'He's a bit of a perfectionist.'

But it is James Hunt who finally comes up with the sort of answer most relevant to our present concerns. Former World Motor Racing Champion, Mr Hunt has been playing squash to a very high standard since he was 18. In the early 70s, he helped Surrey win the County Championship. Ideally, he would devote 'two and a half hours a day' to this 'favourite hobby'. As a winner, he naturally believes in competition:

> 'Victory is important in any game. I play to enjoy it *and* try to win'.

He feels the game offers a unique combination of rewards:

> 'Squash gives you opportunities to display aggression denied in other sports. But immediately after a game of squash, even if you played badly and lost, *then you shouldn't have enough energy to be violently upset*'.

At last we have it. What's so good about squash for men who feel aggressive is that it permits aggression to be explored from start to finish, from arousal to depletion, without causing serious casualties, while even permitting the discharge of stress and provoking a reaction against further violence.

This may be the best we can settle for today. Men will probably continue to believe in the importance of winning, as if the existence of Number One did not *entirely* depend for its reality on the existence of Numbers Two, Three and so forth. It would be infinitely preferable to achieve competitiveness and selflessness simultaneously, like Buddhist ping-pong players, or indeed like many women. It is interesting to note that the intensely demanding and competitive game of badminton grew out of the gentle 'ladies'' game of battledore, in which both players tried to keep a shuttlecock in the air as long as possible. For the one game higher than the game of competition is the game of co-operation. Let us use this as a marker for the future. We might even re-value the language of personal abuse so that 'He who plays like a woman' would be one in receipt of the highest praise. The psychologist Carol Gilligan has pointed out how good it would be for mankind to attempt to behave more like a games-playing girl:

> 'There is a basic difference between the way boys and girls play games. The object of many girls' games is to keep the ball going back and forth. The object of most boys' games is to win whilst the opponent loses. Girls don't want to get involved in winning or losing. They worry about the feelings of the losers. This is a tremendously valuable perspective' (*In A Different Voice: Psychological Theory And Women's Development*, 1982).

This is not intended to be fey. For that you have to share an experience of mine at Los Angeles airport in 1976 when a female astrologer from Arkansas asked me to play chess to pass the time between flights; after the completion of seven moves, she exclaimed in consternation: 'But, good god, you're playing to win!'. I couldn't think of anything suitable to say.

8 Families need Fathers

'My father and I still have no relationship, because of all the years I was growing up when I never really had a father – he was always working, even until late at night and on weekends. I almost never saw him. But I sometimes feel guilty for not accepting the psychological realities of why he did what he did; after all, he provided for us with all the material benefits we could possibly want. I wonder if I shouldn't feel more for my father than I do – I don't feel much, except anger' (quoted by Shere Hite, *The Hite Report on Male Sexuality*, 1981)

'Time should be set aside for family life, for father to be simply a man – not "he who dominates a woman" nor "he who provides" but simply "he, a person who can feel"' (Maureen Green, *Goodbye Father*, 1976)

'I remember thinking with a lot of disgust about small babies. They seemed to be all wet and damp and smelly and dribbling juices of various sorts from one end or the other. I thought, my goodness, how could people do that – looking at these young mothers and thinking it's awful. But once you're actually faced with a shitty nappy that needs changing and you do it . . . the next one isn't a problem.' (John Duffy, *Men . . .*, BBC2, 1984)

It is usually true to say that absent fathers have distant sons, but even those who are present for the fathering process can produce the same result. Fathers who keep their emotional distance broadcast a powerful warning message about the incorrectness of intimacy. This is picked up by both male and female offspring and can produce some of the saddest feelings in any family. In particular, it deprives the fathers themselves of the compensation of finding a secure, in-house personal identity.

Hitherto, the manly stereotype has offered only the role of paid employment to men as a means of self-fulfilment. Sophisticated theories even suggest that by getting on career-wise, men can somehow overcome fears of death. In other words, if intimations of mortality ever trouble the likes of Krupp or Rockefeller or even 'J. R. Ewing' they can be cheered up by the thought that at least their empires are invulnerable. This has never made much sense to me. A company can fire you, even though it's a family holding. A company can retire you before your time. Corporations only endure while they can command cash. And historic family names are constantly being obliterated by the processes of agglomeration. But a father and a mother and a child in a family cannot be retired or fired. You may be able to divorce your husband or wife, but you can never technically divorce your children and vice versa. (Note – attempting to establish fatherly rapport for life with your children is utterly distinct from the *Dombey and Son* syndrome of seeking to found a patriarchal male line.)

Quite by chance, I found myself in conversation with a 60-year-old Gloucestershire house-painter. He was telling me why he favoured early retirement. Suddenly, his face furrowed and he turned the talk in another direction:

> 'Do you know the worst thing in my life was something my son said to me the other day. We're very close he and I and we can say anything we like but there's always been a difference between us and he said: "Dad, when I was a little boy and wanted you to play with me you always said you were too tired or busy" – and do you know, that really hurt because I can never have that time back'.

Dr Joyce Brothers quotes an example of a similar realisation by an American father:

> 'Everything I read convinced me that my wife would have a really tough time when the kids left home. But she didn't. I was the one who almost cracked up.
>
> I had started to let up a little on the time and energy I was devoting to my job. I decided that I had cheated myself. I had not allowed myself time to enjoy my children as they were growing up. They were strangers to me in

some ways. I wanted to get closer to them. But they had no desire or need to get close to me at that time.

When they were little they used to wheedle me to do things with them, but I tried to avoid whatever it was they wanted. Now that I wanted to do things with them, they were too busy with their own lives' (*What Every Woman Should Know About Men*, 1982).

This is pretty close to a form of divorce, I admit, yet there is still a framework of bonds on which the misguided father can attempt to weave new connections.

It only comes to this because all fathers were once sons and many suffered in the process. One of my clients came for counselling because he was a compulsive blusher. He didn't socialise, invite people home or visit the barber – all because he thought it 'unmanly' to blush and to be seen doing so. His loss of confidence was putting terminal strain on his marriage and business. And yet this same man had played tennis professionally, won medals for football, been a fine hurdler and competed successfully at a number of 'male' activities. None of this helped. His father had consistently ignored him, being always too busy proving to the world what a magnificent winner he himself was at selling motor bikes. He failed to teach his boy how to handle himself in company, with women or at a party. The only message the boy got was that he must enter into competitions and win at all costs, but when it came to the social game, no one had told him the rules. He felt awkward. He burned with embarrassment. His face became scarlet. He saw clearly what had happened and thought he knew how others would regard him. Men who don't cry *obviously* don't show shame. They are shame-free, or so he felt his father would think, if his father had been available to articulate the judgement. Today, even his anticipated fear of blushing causes him to blush and in order to get his hair cut (thus avoiding the barber's mirror with its hated reflections) he chooses to pay the man to come to his house:

'It's the most dreadful problem in the world. I'd literally give anything in order to be able not to blush'.

Ironically enough, his problem only came to a head once he'd reached middle years and could no longer obtain masculine reinforcement from racing away with the sporting prizes. When he wasn't able to achieve external victories, he had no choice but to look inwards. What he discovered was intriguing. In all those years of running and jumping on the playing fields, all he had ever really wanted was for his dad to turn up once and say 'Well done'. His dad never did, so he kept on running . . .

It takes time, pain and talent to break the chain of command exhorting each man to follow closely in his father's psychological footsteps. My client was given a negative message, the product of indifference, to avoid emotional closeness. Others, of course, are given a hot positive order to 'replicate Pappy or else'. Often they do. Sometimes, they rebel. Occasionally, their engine of change comes from the specialist workshop of sexual deviance. Witness the story of novelist Edmund White.

White, who is homosexual, held his father in abhorrence. He was told to be 'like his father' although he could not conform to his heterosexual expectations. These were closely enmeshed with the Senior White's definition of masculinity. Junior White began to gain perspective on Senior White's world-view, eventually depicting this in an admittedly autobiographical novel first published in 1982. Here then is how it feels to be the modern son of a rejecting father:

'He was the one with the power, the money, the right to read the paper through dinner as my stepmother and I watched him in silence; he was the one with the thirty tailor-made suits, the twenty gleaming pairs of shoes and the starched white dress shirts, the ties from Countess Mara and the two cadillacs that waited for him in the garage, dripping oil on the concrete in the shape of a black Saturn and its gray blur of moons. It was his power that stupefied me and made me regard my knowledge as nothing more than hired cleverness he might choose to show off at a dinner party ("Ask this young fellow, he reads, he'll know") . . .

'My sister was his true son. She could ride a horse and swim a mile and she was as capable of sustained rages as he . . . "I don't think you should talk about your mother that way, young fellow, she's a fine woman".

"But, Daddy", I exclaimed, my voice breaking and rising up, up the scale into a soprano delirium, "I *love* my mother".

"Like. Like." he said. "A man likes things. Girls love, men like" . . .

'For my father, sitting uncomfortably in that petit-point chair without arms, manliness was not discussable, but had it been, it would have included a good business suit, ambition, paying one's bills on time, enough knowledge of baseball to hand out like tips at the barbershop, a residual but never foolhardy degree of courage, and an unbreachable reserve . . . Women lived for love and talked about it and made their decisions by its guttering, scented light; men (at least real men like my dad) took the love that came their way gratefully but suffered its absence in silence. Certainly no real man ever discussed love or made a single move to woo it . . .

'My father didn't like other men; he had no close male friends and he behaved towards the men in his own family according to the dictates of duty rather than the impulses of his heart. He so often ascribed cunning to other men, a covert plotting, that he approached them as enemies to whom he must extend an ambiguous hand, one that when not offering a cold greeting could contract into a fist. I was one of the men he didn't like' (Edmund White, *A Boy's Own Story*, 1982).

I have quoted this at length because, regardless of White's sexual orientation, I believe it makes the point that the manly stereotype has done damage in depriving both fathers *and* sons of emotional pleasures and rewards. In some families, of course, the rejections have gone even further. The late Dr Howard Brown (in *Familiar Faces, Hidden Lives*, 1976) tells the tale of one son who for his graduation present was given 25 dollars by his father, driven to the station, put on the train to New York and informed: 'I hope I never hear from you again'. A peculiar interpretation of the duties of paternity, especially from one who also happened to be a minister of the gospel.

Underlying this response is the strange heresy that paternity is optional – as if fatherhood were something that men can take up or not, as and when they please. If traditional masculine values lead us in that direction, then it is high time to announce that men will lose more than they gain. Every ageing father who, like King Lear, banishes his child really does so from a position of weakness. He is the declining power, his progeny the rising one and in his years of infirmity, the father needs the child immeasurably more than the child needs him.

The notion of optional paternity is defiantly engrained into male chauvinism. One of the characters in a Joe Orton play tells his sister she should think herself lucky that the father was present at the conception, let alone the birth. A recent *New Society* article described the attitudes of one young criminal Londoner:

> 'I wanted to see if it was a boy or girl before marrying her. If it had been a girl, I might not have bothered' ('The Hoxton Creeper Who Can't Go Straight', *New Society*, 18/8/1983).

This attitude reflects the widespread view that the verb 'to father' refers to little more than the spasm of ejaculation. The law has historically supported such partiality. Even today, the courts will generally equate parenting with motherhood and impregnation with paternity. As a result, in some 70 to 80 per cent of divorce cases, custody is awarded to the mother. No more than one in 10 husbands will challenge this ruling and consequently many divorce cases spell the end, or at least the demise of a relationship between the child and one of its parents, almost invariably the father.

Such legal bias against fatherhood is supported by outmoded theories on the psychology of motherhood. Since the war, the prevailing childcare assumptions have been matriarchal:

> 'The seminal work of the new matriarchy was John Bowlby's study *Maternal Care and Maternal Health* (1951). Bowlby acknowledged that fathers and siblings play an important part in a child's upbringing, but a well adjusted adult could only be guaranteed in the future if the child had been subjected to total, warm, unbroken mothering, preferably with the same person. Studies of total mothering followed Bowlby in their hundreds' ('Don't Fathers Have Rights Too?', *Sunday Times*, 9/3/1980).

At the professional psychological level, however, it is now better understood that:

> 'A less exclusive focus on mothers is required. Children also have fathers' (Michael Rutter, *Maternal Deprivation Reassessed*, 1972).

It is also known that children can adapt to more than one 'nurturant' adult. The current view is that up to five such adults of either sex may be the 'supportive parent figures' for almost any given child up to the age of five (Professor Martin Richards, Cambridge University).

Even those in support of traditional values concede there is no evidence to suggest that males have any *inborn* tendency to be poor at parenting. Studies by Bem, Parke and O'Leary show that fathers are just as good at playing with newborn babies and coping with infant wants as mothers. In one experiment, they behaved more nurturantly than the mothers did when both parents were present, and they were at least as nurturant when they were alone with the child (quoted by Tavris and Offir, *The Longest War: Sex Differences in Perspective*, 1977). These findings are also confirmed (insofar as such things are relevant) by tests on rhesus monkeys where the males can be coaxed into becoming impeccable 'mothers' in the laboratory. And for those who pick up on the word *coax*, bear in mind that the so-called human *maternal* instinct has almost always been at the mercy of social custom. In a preponderance of societies, mothers have committed infanticide to rid themselves of the shame or burden of unwanted offspring:

'Great numbers of Victorian women, in the heyday of the female ideal, killed their own illegitimate children . . .' (Tavris and Offir, 1977).

If males need coaxing into greater nurturance, so sometimes do women.

From society's standpoint, fathers can only opt out of fatherhood at the price of family instability. In the nuclear family, an absent or distant father unbalances the structure in favour of the mother. She may become anti-sex and anti-men, which sometimes encourages sexual guilt in boys. She will certainly bear the full burden of responsibility for discipline. If she copes, the child will associate punishment with women. If she doesn't, the child will find personal growth difficult since no boundary against which to measure him/herself will have been established. Ideally, the child will have learned where the boundaries of acceptable behaviour are both for males and females *from* both males and females.

From the child's perspective, what should prevent the *actual* father (as well as the *actual* mother) from opting out of the parenting role is the reasonable desire we all have to know where we come from. It really shouldn't have to be spelled out, but it takes two people to make a third, which actually means that we require to be in regular touch with the parents who created us. This is not a question of ancestor-worship through the male line as some have suggested. We need to stock up a full memory in order to establish personal identity. To that end, at the simplest level, girls and boys must be taught to feel comfortable with the bodies and personalities belonging to both the sexes. Ideally, their blood parents will be their teachers even though they may share the 'nurturing' roles between them. A child gains most security from having an adult version of itself on tap for comparisons, attachments and rejections, sexual or otherwise.

The implication of this is a far cry from the legal view of fatherhood as impregnation. The second and most important part of the paternal concept extends fathering and masculinity to cover all the emotional aspects of child-rearing. This in turn entails a formal revolution in the hitherto unbalanced lives of men. In one study in America, they were timed and it was found (to everyone's stupefaction) that the average US father spends just 12 minutes per day with his children. One immediate effect of this is to over-emphasise the masculine 'presence' around the house almost in terms of its physical 'absence'. Father is seen as that distant disciplinarian. His legislation is handed down and frequently resented. Boys in particular find his behaviour hard to stomach since it is *their* parent – the one *like them* – who is dealing with them at arm's length. Sometimes, having a reserved or uninvolved father is equivalent to having none. The same is true if the father adds himself to his wife's list of children who need mothering, or even, like some insidious cuckoo, demands all her attention for himself.

When the father declines to adjust himself to his children's imaginative level, communication is prevented. Fathers of this type sound like a book of rules and many of their injunctions are self-contradictory. Again, it is sons who seem to suffer most. The clearest example is the conflict inherent in the twin commands 'obey your father' and 'make your own decisions'. In case you don't already know, it is very difficult to do as you are told while standing on your own two feet. Since these messages travel from an emotional distance, boys especially form an unguided notion of the limits of personal reality. If a father appears to be telling his son to go West and achieve great things, how can the son be blamed for commencing to live on wish-fulfilment:

'Perhaps this is why so many men learn to exaggerate their

own success: heroes in the end die hard' (Andrew Tolson, *The Limits of Masculinity*, 1977).

When we get down to it, fathering is not just a matter of discipline or even childcare. The real burden is infinitely heavier. It means commitment. The decision to become a parent seems to me to be elementally more significant than making up your mind whether or not to get married. From marriage there is divorce. You've only damaged yourself and another grown-up. From parenting, there is no parole for the 16 or so years it will take your child to learn to function independently. You are obliged during that time to be present both in body and mind, however tough things get, because the inexcusable alternative is to damage the innocent.

The immediate reward is to establish a happy personal intimacy with the new generation, which in the longer term will improve your chances of developing an adult version of the skill invaluable in your relations with peers. At present, the arrival of children causes a marked deterioration in the quality of the relationship between their parents. This is not inevitable. The principal cause is attempting to do too much on too few human resources. It is not possible to have children and to be a workaholic during their early years. This applies to women as well as men. You both must choose which matters most. Nor is it possible for husbands (or wives) to remain the centre of attention once the children are born. Before you embark on producing a family, you must decide whether psychologically you can afford to put yourself last – or at least last but one – in the pecking order. Since men derive so much gratification from working, the question is sometimes one and the same as asking if you can let your career mark time for a few years.

This is not an over-idealistic view. In fact, there is little alternative. Women are no longer keen on the 'marriage of one-handed parenthood'. Another of my clients has painfully separated from her husband only because he always puts the business first. He is a reasonable and active father when he is around. But he is only around after nine p.m. when his daughter is asleep and on those weekends when he doesn't jet to France and the USA. He is generous with his cash; doesn't chase other women; doesn't get violent and has absolutely no idea why his marriage isn't working. He loves his wife and misses her. The most difficult part for her to cope with is his ignorance of the problem. He cannot see what other people constantly need –

attention, time, togetherness. This brings home the fact that he cannot begin to relate to her and his child.

Contrast this case with that of Mr Ian McNab of Primrose Hill, North London, who was granted clearance by his local council to adopt a child even though he is a single man of 44. He can fit this in quite easily with his work as a typographic designer, largely because he is based at home:

> 'I purposely set up my work at home . . . so that there would always be someone on hand when the children got home from school'

and the local council commented:

> '. . . it is individuals who make good parents, not sex. A good parent needs that little bit extra and Mr McNab has it. He is prepared to put himself out and identify with the needs of children' (*Hampstead & Highgate Express*, 11/8/1978).

The biggest pay-off for men who copy Mr McNab and devote care to fathering will come from breaking that chain of command which teaches boys to be emotionally closed. Being part of a family is then fun. This fun will ultimately alter the world. It will amount to a bloodless *coup d'état* literally against the present state of being. It will alter the battle of the sexes irrevocably. The children of the future can grow up without having to model their mentalities on the dichotomy between authoritarian fathers and permissive mothers. Instead, parents and children will be able to remain in touch as a unit in which males are accepted in the nurturing, emotionally giving role just as readily as females. In fact, it is already happening:

> 'In the exigencies of modern middle class living what I see around me is interchangeability. The roles (of mother and father) change according to the most efficient way of living . . . As a broad generalisation the children tend to look first to the parent from whom they would expect to receive whatever it is that they want but easily turn to the other if deprived or thwarted' (Alex Scarr, *Guardian*, 8/5/1980).

Such interchangeability of role between father and mother does not mean that the differences of personality between them will be erased, nor does it mean that their different skills will be undervalued. If one is to have two parents it is clearly desirable that they should not be pale reflections of each other. But there is little justification in making mother the permanent cook nor in appointing father the permanent chauffeur. The same goes for giving comfort and discipline. If these roles are stereotyped by parents along sexual lines, it gives children the handicap of not being able to cross tracks: how will males *ever* get fed in the new feminist age if they don't start to master the simplicities of a pot roast and sole *bonne femme* themselves? However, a special relationship will probably always remain between the parent and child who share the same biological sex; and, like all things human, it will probably consist in equal parts of love and hate.

If this is the new fatherhood, beware of imitations. There are men around who want the rewards of intimate paternity without working for them. If their desire is frustrated, they can behave just like the wicked Victorian paterfamilias who, resentful of the mother's closer ties, would order his wife to 'make the children respect him'. The genuine article must possess the following virtues (perceptively summarised by Sheila Macleod in 'Men Will Be Boys', *Guardian*, 7/6/1982):

'● altruism (your needs come second when another life depends on you)
● persistence (sticking to the task even though the reward is deferred)
● intuition (reviving the masculine version of this – learning how to perceive and anticipate the child's moods – e.g. realising the boy/girl is not being bloody-minded when it refuses to go to bed and creating a coping strategy that does not rely on force to manoeuvre it between the sheets)
● unconditional love (one that does not require a *quid pro quo*)
● teaching morality (giving the child the opportunity to see the existence of choices and the consequence of its actions. Perhaps the most widely neglected of the fathering virtues today)'.

One of the gravest difficulties men have with parenting is the impossibility of crowning the work with any success. Men are culturally and emotionally biased towards victory and yet with raising children you are undertaking a no-win task. Whatever you do as a parent will lead to (some) failure. As I am by no means the first to point out, the only interesting question remaining is *how* you fail. In fathering there are no guaranteed rewards, no signposts, no infallible precedents. Curiously enough, it begins to sound like a competitive man's idea of the ultimate challenge. For that's what it is: the world's only impossible task. I am almost surprised more masculine men don't take it on.

The crunch comes of course with adolescence when, in order for the children to attain their new individuality, parents must collude in their own displacement. The psychologist Winnicott goes so far as to call this process the symbolic *murder* of parents by their offspring. Typically, this is the moment when a great number of fathers choose to undergo their own crisis and drop out of parenting altogether. They cannot accept rejections. They feel emotionally lost. They suspect the only answer for them is a renewal of their own adolescence, minus adult responsibilities. That was the last time they themselves felt really powerful. And they still believe that only *external* power can provide balm. It is at this time that fathers scream at teenage daughters about un-desirable boyfriends and show their brutal sides to sons who dare to challenge their moral and political authority. Many fathers actually walk out. But it is precisely at this moment that the young adolescent needs supportive care: needs the father to take (on the chin) the ritual blows delivered; to endure them and transcend them in order to endorse the child's pre-adult autonomy. And to find the *internal* power to manage this. As one of my adolescent correspondents puts it:

'I am 17 and since a long time ago me and my dad haven't got on. We don't seem to be able to talk together for five minutes without rowing. I say one remark and he begins to shout or lecture, going on and on. He can't seem to let a subject rest. For him discussing something means him giving orders and me obeying them. I realise that some-times he is right. He is older than I am and more experi-enced in the world but he seems to think that the only opinions I am allowed to have are his. Anything else is regarded as trendy leftish rubbish. For instance, when I was in the third year it was suggested that I might like to pick sociology as an option. He got so angry that my mum had to stand between me and him to prevent him from hit-ting me. I wasn't even considering the subject. He asked me what the school had said and I had told him. He just blew his top.

The latest incident was on Sunday. I had been reading *The Double Helix* and had left the book on a chair. Dad came in and asked me what I thought of it. I said that I thought it was quite good, interesting, but sexist in parts. I was going to say that Watson made up for it at the end by apologising to women and listing some of their scientific achievements. But he didn't let me get that far. He got really cross saying it was a scientific book about the discovery of DNA (like I hadn't read it) and suggesting I didn't deserve to look at a copy . . .'

Immediately I see here the opportunity of establishing a very rewarding friendship with a highly intelligent new adult being lost by a peremptory parent.

I would probably not have been able to see any such thing but for acquiring three sons of my own, two of them part-time step-children. If I am honest, they have been the most formative factor in my adult life to date, more important to me than university scholarships, intellectual discovery, work or sex. They have helped me to recognise feelings I didn't know I possessed. They have made me feel vulnerable in a way that frightens me yet makes me taste life more strongly. I have learned something of the importance of self-sacrifice. If only one person could be rescued from our blazing family house, I now think I could manage to make it somebody other than me. I have learned that a child has a decisive personality of his own from birth and that you cannot make a child in your own image. In any case, it is not a question of giving children instruction so much as *learning* how to teach them by observing their behaviour. I've learned something about one-way love for the first time in my life, not looking for pay-offs, but enjoying what comes to me. I've learned to be available even when working:

'Dad, can we do things together today since I haven't spent a lot of time with you lately?'

to which the answer is 'Yes', although I have by no means finished my 'little bit of work'. Over and above all this, I have learned something about my own childhood, about those years between the ages of nought and four forgotten by me, and about the effort and care my own father and mother must have put into looking after me. It has completed the rest of my story by allowing me to 'imagine my own prologue' – a process humbling but helpful.

All in all, I feel relatively comfortable about having sired my own 'replacement' and I am sure this is initially to do with having been present at his birth. He is not a visitation from another planet nor a medical discovery made in the laboratory of the West London Hospital. He actually came down his mother's birth canal to my certain knowledge. I don't see how a father can form easy attachments to a being whose very existence transcends his own experience. Until you have watched it, the making of flesh *from* flesh must remain beyond belief and the offspring an outsider.

The subsequent business of child-rearing now seems to me to offer men a job so demanding that it shapes a whole adult life with its limitations and responsibilities. I think it means becoming a different person, less free on the surface because more connected underneath. The new fatherhood offers men access to their previously unpermitted feelings of empathy and altruism. It extends masculinity almost for the first time to cover the idea of duty to nurture – to touch your sons and daughters, to comfort them when they're hurt, to cook for them, to look after them when they are ill, to learn from them. It thus offers society a possibly unwelcome social revolution by giving men a mature relevance at home to accompany their relevance in the wider world of work. Yet if we don't grab this opportunity we shall remain without any convincing defence to the charge that we ourselves cannot grow up:

> 'The lesson the [father] . . . is imparting to his children is that the male of the species can do as he pleases while the female is the repository of adult responsibility; that parenting is mainly a matter for women, who can be discarded once they have outlived their usefulness; and that fatherhood is a kind of game, of which you can say, when you feel threatened by defeat, "I'm not playing any more".
>
> Persistence, altruism, intuitive responsiveness, the ability to postpone [some types of] gratification, the inculcation of morals. All these are seen as intrinsically feminine values, which can therefore be downgraded. But they are not intrinsically feminine. They are intrinsically adult. Oh yes, boys will be boys, all right. If only men would learn to be men' (Macleod, *Guardian*, 7/6/1982).

9 Memo to Self

> 'Here have we literary and cultured persons been for years setting up a cry of the New Woman . . . and never noticing the advent of the New Man' (George Bernard Shaw, *Man and Superman*, 1903)

In the battle of the sexes nowadays, it is men's behaviour that appears to be anachronistic. We are an old-fashioned conscript army ever eager to obey our leaders' orders and I daresay we could do a passable imitation of the goosestep upon request. In our steel skulls, we are enclosed. We are noisy. We always seek out prominence. We automatically hit those who hurt us as if that makes our hurt any the less. We don't hesitate to kill when challenged on our chosen ego-ground, be it philosophy, politics or economics. In the world at large, screens beam us daily pictures from fresh killing zones of young warriors in identical poses exulting in their male lethality. Some 50 millions have died at the hands of psychiatrically normal males since 1900. We are the death sex. Men say they fight for a cause, but that cause is their own identity, an external source of power, which they cannot find in themselves. The wars of virility are without end since those who learn nothing from history's errors are doomed to repeat them in a cycle of tragedy and farce.

At home, at peace, we witness the quieter rituals of masculine self-defence. Men, it seems, would rather do anything than let their fellows catch a glimpse of their feelings. At the trivial level, we hold in our hearts a sort of national 'Pseuds' Corner', a place of opprobrium to which we commit anyone who goes emotionally over the top. Then we can giggle our fears of sentiment away. We seem to believe that repression of feelings is preferable to their expression, although we know that emotional denial distorts the personality. The man who spends his time deriding as 'pseuds' those who display their emotions is only delaying the day when, in the language of psychotherapy, his own 'internal adult' will cry out for love and affection. Until then, he is locked in the rudimentary belief structures of adolescence:

> 'There is only one God; and the Captain of School is His Prophet.
> My school is the best in the world.
> Without big muscles, strong will and proper collars there is no salvation . . .
> I must play games with all my heart, with all my soul and with all my strength . . .
> Enthusiasm, except for games, is in bad taste.
> I must look up to the older fellows and pour contempt on newcomers.
> I must show no emotion and not kiss mother in public'
> (taken from the *Ten Commandments of the Public Schoolboy*, quoted by Aland Sandison, *Wheel of Empire*, 1967).

In more serious contexts, we have the police and law courts continuing to define violence to the person *only* as a process of bruising flesh with flesh or some other weapon, as if violence to a person's feelings were not equally offensive:

> 'He covered her face with a nightie, raped her and then fled. Police said the woman was shaken but unhurt' (Court report, *Birmingham Evening Mail*).

> 'Passing sentence, Judge Anthony Goodall told Blackmore: 'You seized this woman, whom you had never met, dragged her off to a quiet spot and raped her. It is the plain duty of the court to protect women from men like you.
>
> All that can be said in your favour is that no real violence was used or threatened' (Court report, *Devon Express and Echo*).

This attitude is unforgiveable towards the rape victims who have suffered a trauma men rarely experience, but it also speaks volumes concerning men's callousness towards emotions in general. For, if seizing a stranger, dragging her off to a quiet spot and raping her entails neither the use nor threat of any *real* violence, then we cannot be speaking about people at all but a species of machines. What men incidentally reveal about themselves can be made explicit. What they are saying in plain terms is:

> 'I, as a man, am never hurt unless you wound me bodily; my feeling of inordinate personal security will never be breached by any treatment you care to mete out unless it also includes physical duress'

to which the only conceivable retort is 'Nuts!'

The range of denied emotions which men feel begins with jealousy (for which they will commit murder) and ends with hubris (for which they will commit 'bitchery' – another of those masculine traits normally ascribed to females). Which sex, when confronted with adultery, more often reaches for the gun and then demands the excusing prerogative of the *crime passionel* if not the overly emotional male? And which sex, when needled, has come up with the most sadistic one-liners against both sexes if not the overly sensitive male? Consider Evelyn Waugh's 'humanitarian' comment when Randolph Churchill had to have a lung excised:

> 'A typical triumph of modern science to find the only part of Randolph that is not malignant and remove it',

which itself was built on Lloyd-George's tasty quip about a political rival:

> 'When they circumcised Lord Samuel they threw the wrong bit away . . .'.

These emotions that men are at such pains to deny deprive them of intimacy and dilute their social intercourse to the extent that those they call friends are really no more than acquaintances. A cousin of mine was talking to me recently about a couple of his friends, whom he sees some two or three times a year. The first friend invited him to his wedding, even though it was a 'small family affair', while the second apparently describes him as his 'best friend'. My cousin was delighted, naturally, to be asked to celebrate a marriage, and pleased to hear that his second chum regards him so fondly. And yet . . . and yet . . . he feels puzzled, 'You see, I see my *best* friend every day', he explained.

If I am honest, both these men, whom I have met, strike me as somewhat guarded and inward-looking with a reserve that is hard to crack. All I know about them is that both attended boarding school from an early age and both have a fairly frozen relationship with their parents, fathers in particular. As long ago as 1945, Spitz (*Psychoanalytic Study of the Child*) found that infants deprived of parental handling over a long period will tend to sink into a decline. Possibly this is why these two men do not even realise how much they lack the skills of intimacy.

It is important for all men to become aware, as Dr Eric Berne noted in 1964 (*Games People Play*), that emotional deprivation can be fatal and that:

> '[The observation] gives rise to the idea of "stimulus-hunger" and indicates that the most favoured forms of stimuli are those provided by physical intimacy, a conclusion not hard to accept on the basis of everyday experience'.

Those who remain isolated from intimacy begin to suffer the symptoms of sensory deprivation:

> 'Experimentally, such deprivation may [even] call forth a transient psychosis, or at least give rise to temporary mental disturbances . . . On the biological side, it is probably that emotional and sensory deprivation tends to bring about or encourage organic changes. If the reticular activating system of the brain stem is not sufficiently stimulated, degenerative changes in the nerve cells may follow . . . a biological chain may be postulated leading from emotional and sensory deprivation through apathy to degenerative changes and death. In this sense, stimulus-hunger has the same relationship to survival of the human organism as food hunger . . . "If you are not stroked, your spinal cord will shrivel up"' (Berne, 1964).

Such a warning seems clear enough. Men are currently cutting off their noses to spite their faces. In Dr Berne's view, the remedy is equally clear. Men must enter into true intimacy with women and other men while indulging in fewer competitive games and rituals:

> '. . . pastimes and games are substitutes for the real living of real intimacy . . . Intimacy begins when individual . . .

programming becomes more intense, and both social pat-
terning and ulterior restrictions and motives begin to give
way. It is the only completely satisfying answer to stimulus
hunger, recognition hunger and structure hunger' (Berne,
1964).

And so we return to our central theme: men who repudiate all
emotional dependency actually increase their emotional needs
and related hungering. They want to be stimulated, recognised
and find a pattern to their lives. But the harder such men strive
for independence, the more they lack self-sufficiency. They are
thwarted. The more they resist affection, the more they crave it.
Sometimes, they try to buy it but the time always runs out with
the money. Frequently, they seek sex in order to get affection but
sex is all they get when they decline to offer affection in return.
As long as men remain emotionally withdrawn, their desires will
continue to be confusing and, frankly, irrational.

Let us try to summarise the position as succinctly as possible,
including the suggested remedies, in a format particularly intel-
ligible to men, written from the outside looking in, as a business
memo:

Memorandum

● Male chauvinism is a defence mechanism. Men ridicule
women because they are frightened of them. They are intimidated by a woman's difference from themselves. They also feel
very disturbed by the existence of female qualities in themselves.
They are psychologically in awe of mothers, beginning with their
own.

● Men are the super-sensitive sex. They feel threatened because they are unable to admit that anything has gone wrong.
Men are getting hurt and won't accept it.

● Men are biologically less successful than women. They die
earlier and remain more vulnerable to stress both biologically
and culturally.

● Men are socially in need of stable relationships. They are
saner and longer-lived when married than when single. Yet men
are currently being criticised, rejected and divorced by women.

● Men are poor at intimacy, at supplying the necessary
emotional sensitivity in relationships, but it is in their interests to

develop this skill with others and with themselves. Modern marriage now depends solely on the ability of the man and the woman to make each other emotionally comfortable together. In addition, men fail to ameliorate their own stress-related problems because they are out of touch with their emotions. Therefore, ultimately, they increase their own pain.

● Men only need to change a little to gain great improvements in their relationships but they falsely see this change as considerable and resist it.

● Power is the key idea. Men go out into the world to seek potency but almost all of them return disappointed. Some become mentally and physically impotent. Their error began in childhood when they first came to believe that power was an extension of muscular force, an action outside the body. On the contrary, true power is inside, is self-power.

● Put it all another way: the rules of the power-game have changed. Women are gaining equality with men. Society has chosen to requisition their skills. If a man wants to retain an effective role for himself in relation to others, it makes no sense to cling to a role-definition dependent on male supremacy. He has to admit visitors to his mental palace, keep fewer secrets, pursue open dialogue, permit himself to become vulnerable to criticism, admit doubt. How else is he to learn?

● Admitting doubt provides the strength to resolve it. Men would do well to follow Freud's model of seeking to make their unconscious conscious. The feeling of threat would recede in the tide of awareness.

● This is the pay-off. By reconnecting yourself to the source of inner fear you actually acquire true power for the first time in your life, becoming *genuinely* attractive and impressive in the process. If you don't reveal such feelings, nobody can get close to you or like you.

● Why, after all, do women appreciate problem-laden men such as alcoholics, gamblers and rakes? It is not because women are natural masochists. It is because in the absence of anything better, women will always feel more attracted to men who bare their souls than to men whose hearts are bricked up.

● The foregoing argument is a recipe for men to:
live longer
suffer less stress
enjoy improved relationships with women, children and other men.

● The consequence is for men to gain:
real power
affection and effectiveness
balance and adulthood.

● Social conditions make this mandatory:

'The key to survival in the nuclear age is going to be perception, the ability to sense how others feel about an event or issue or a threat and what they are likely to do about it' (Brothers, 1982).

● The only question remaining is whether men *want* to survive.

For men seeking help with problems at work or in relationships
a brief address list is available. It will also include some sugges-
tions for further reading and can be obtained from:

> Men . . .
> BBC
> London W12 8QT.

Further Reading

The following books have all been read by me with profit:

Bengis, Ingrid *Combat in the Erogenous Zone* (Wildwood House, 1972).

Brothers, Dr Joyce *What Every Woman Should Know About Men* (Simon & Schuster, 1981; Granada, 1982).

Chesler, Phyllis *About Men* (Simon and Schuster, 1978).

Figes, Eva *Patriarchal Attitudes* (Faber & Faber, 1970).

Gilligan, Carol *In A Different Voice: Psychological Theory and Women's Development* (Harvard University Press, 1982).

Green, Maureen *Goodbye Father* (Routledge and Kegan Paul, 1976).

Hite, Shere *The Hite Report On Male Sexuality* (Alfred A. Knopf, 1981).

Hooper, Anne *Divorce and Your Children* (Allen and Unwin, 1981).

Lazarre, Jane *On Loving Men* (Virago, 1981).

Maccoby, Eleanor and Jacklin, Carol *The Psychology of Sex Differences*, (Stanford University Press, 1974).

Oakley, Ann *Sex, Gender and Society* (Temple Smith, 1972).

Rowbotham, Sheila *Woman's Consciousness, Man's World* (Pelican, 1973).

Synner, Robin and Cleese, John *Families and How to Survive Them* (Methuen, 1983).

Tavris, Carol and Offir, Carole *The Longest War: Sex Differences in Perspective* (Harcourt Brace Jovanovich, 1977).

Tolson, Andrew *The Limits of Masculinity* (Tavistock Publications, 1977).

Willis, Paul *Learning to Labour* (Saxon House, 1977).

Zilbergeld, Bernie *Men and Sex* (Souvenir Press, 1979).

Excerpts from Brothers (1982), Caro (*The Years of Lyndon Johnson*: Alfred A. Knopf 1982; Collins 1983), Hite (1981), Tavris and Offir (1977) and White (*A Boy's Own Story*: E. P. Dutton 1982; Pan Books 1983) were reprinted by permission of the publishers.